5

PORTRAIT OF THE CLYDE

OTHER BOOKS BY JACK HOUSE

Portrait of
THE CLYDE

JACK HOUSE

ILLUSTRATED AND WITH MAP

ROBERT HALE · LONDON

SBN 7091 4994 8

Robert Hale & Company
63 Old Brompton Road
London S.W.7

Printed and bound in Great Britain by
REDWOOD BURN LIMITED
Trowbridge & Esher

CONTENTS

ILLUSTRATIONS

PICTURE CREDITS

CHAPTER I

THE ELUSIVE RIVER

The River Clyde, flowing some one hundred miles from the
Lowther Hills to the city of Glasgow and then down to the most
beautiful estuary in the world, has a somewhat varied reputation.
To the majority of people furth of Scotland it has been known as a
shipbuilding centre. To some it is still, politically, the 'Red Clyde'.
To many a veteran of the last war—American, French, Polish,
Norwegian—the Clyde is an entrance to hospitality.

To Glaswegians the Clyde is a sort of sacred river, and the
famous local bromide has it that "Glasgow made the Clyde, and
the Clyde made Glasgow". This is true in a commercial sense, but
it has given rise to the idea that Glasgow was founded on the
River Clyde. As I shall show later, that is not the case. The
founders of the original Glasgow did not take the Clyde into their
considerations at all.

The trouble with the Clyde is that if you first set eyes on it
from, say, Glasgow Bridge, it doesn't look like an important
river. In breadth, at this point, it is hardly half that of the Thames
at Westminster Bridge. It has the same dark grey look, even in
bright sunshine. And, though it widens considerably as it flows
towards the sea, it is still narrow by the standards of other rivers.

When the Cunarder *Queen Mary*, then the biggest ship ever
made, was to be launched from John Brown's shipyard at Clydebank, an English guest (a shipbuilder himself) was heard to
wonder how it was possible to get such a giant afloat on "that
trout stream".

Dr. George Pratt Insh, one of the most eminent historians of
Glasgow University, called the Clyde "the elusive river". He

9

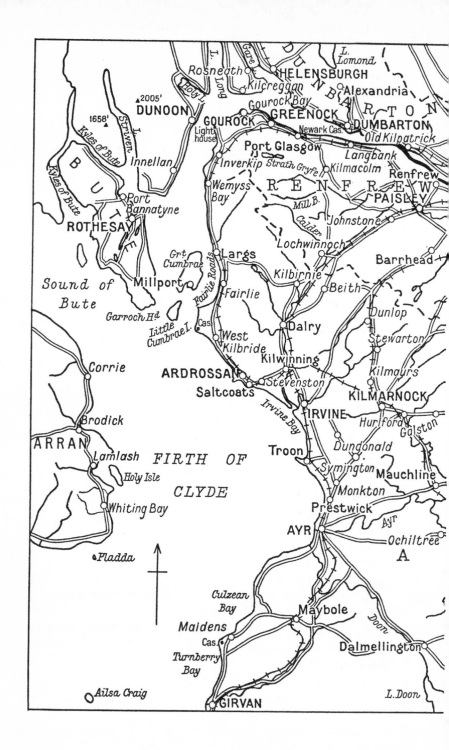

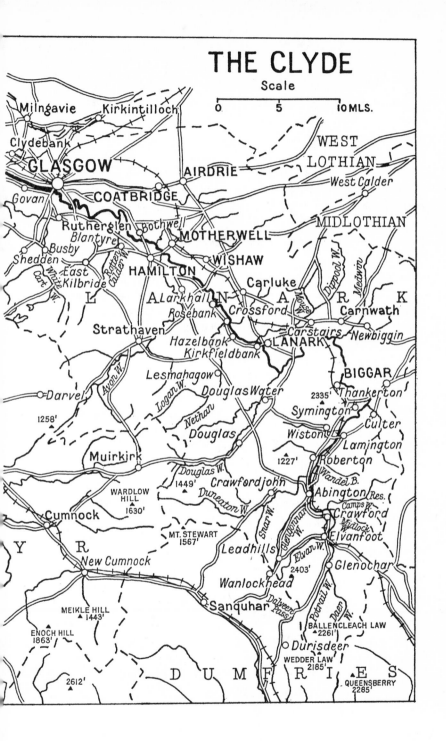

meant that in its upper reaches from the source to very near Glasgow, it was difficult to find without trespassing into private estates or risking life and limb on steep banks or penetrating steelworks and other industrial complexes. Certainly the industrialists who settled along the banks of the river in the nineteenth century regarded it as a mere utility.

Around 1840 a book was published in Scotland with the delightful title of "*Strath-Clutha, or the Beauties of the Clyde. Delineated in a series of Views of the Principal Towns and Villages, Watering Places, Palaces, Castles and Gentlemen's Seats and Romantic Scenery*, by John M. Leighton, Esqr. Joseph Swan, Engraver."

Mr. Leighton wrote:

Among the rivers of Scotland, the Clyde is usually ranked as the third. But when we consider the riches of the coal and mineral districts through which it flows; the various valuable manufactures carried on upon its banks; the extended commerce which its towns possess, with every portion of the habitable globe; and the energy, activity and ingenuity of their inhabitants; we are justly entitled to hold it as the most important of Scottish streams.

Of course, Mr. Leighton was taking the Victorian view that industrial development was the way to Paradise. He was more interested in the river as it ran through the Black Country of Motherwell, Wishaw and Hamilton to Glasgow and its shipyards, and then down to the "watering places" which were just being developed by rich merchants at that time. But he did quote a Mr. Cyril Thornton who was impressed by the upper reaches of the river sufficiently to write, "I had never seen before and I have never seen since, any river which, for natural beauty, can stand in competition with the Clyde. Never did stream glide more gracefully to the ocean through a fairer region."

The poet's view was rather different. Thomas Campbell, who wrote "Rule Britannia" among other things, was a Glasgow man, and, after some time in London, came back to his native city and was so appalled that he wrote:

> My native Clyde, thy once romantic shore
>   Where nature's face is banished and estranged
> And Heaven reflected in thy wave no more.

Obviously Campbell was born too late. We have the testimony of William Lithgow of Lanark that the Clyde in the seventeenth century was a place of rare beauty. Mr. Lithgow was known as 'Lugless Will' because he had had his ears cut off in his youth for what the late Neil Munro called "injudicious gallantry". After this episode Lugless Will left Lanark and travelled through Europe, the Levant and Northern Africa.

One night on a Grecian island he stood in a small creek awaiting in dread an attack by Turks, and, in order to keep his mind off possible events, he composed a poem which, when the attack did not materialize, he wrote down. Here it is, and if you don't think much of its quality please recollect the conditions under which it was composed:

> Would God I might but live
> To see my native soil,
> Twice happy is my happy wish
> To end this endless toil.
>
> Yet still would I record
> The pleasant banks of Clyde,
> Where orchards, castles, towns and woods
> Are planted side by side;
>
> And chiefly Lanark thou
> Thy country's lowest Lamp
> In which the bruised body now
> Did first receive the stamp.

Neil Munro himself, writing in 1907, described the Clyde as "the most astonishing, beautiful and inspiring of Scottish waterways". He said it was really three rivers in one, since it combined the quiet river, the industrial river and the beautiful river.

And that is still true, more than sixty years later. Myself, I have twice walked every step of the one hundred miles from the Broomielaw harbour in Glasgow to the source of the Clyde. I have spent a lifetime on its banks, both above and below Glasgow. If you can really know a river, I think I know it as well as any man.

I recollect what Sir Walter Scott wrote in *Rob Roy*, when that great man, Bailie Nicol Jarvie of Glasgow, on his travels through the Highlands found himself on the banks of a narrow, deep and silent river. "That's the Forth", he remarked and he did so, according to Mr. Francis Osbaldistone, "with an air of reverence which I have observed the Scotch usually pay to their distinguished rivers. The Clyde, the Tweed, the Forth, the Spey are named by those who dwell on their banks with a sort of respect and pride."

So, without the slightest difficulty, I summon up my respect and pride and take you to the beginnings of the River Clyde.

CHAPTER II

THE SOURCES OF THE CLYDE

I doubt if any river in Britain can have had so many suggested
sources as the Clyde. When I started school, getting on for fifty
years ago, we were told, in a general sort of way, that the River
Clyde rose by Tinto Hill. Since from various elevations round
Glasgow we could see Tinto, we were most impressed.

Later I learned, on what I took to be real authority, that the
source was the Little Clyde Burn on Beattock Summit, not far
from where the railway is the link between Scotland and England.
This source seemed well documented. In the early eighteenth
century a Dr. Pennecuick wrote:

The famous Tweed hath its first spring or fountain nearly a mile to
the east of the place where the shire of Peebles marches and borders
with the stewartry of Annandale—that is Tweed's Cross. Both
Annan and Clyde have their first rise from the same height, about
half a mile from one another, where Clyde runneth west, Annan to
the south and Tweed to the east.

Perhaps Dr. Pennecuick was taking as gospel an ancient rhyme
in the district:

Annan, Tweed and Clyde
Rise on ae hillside

There are various versions of this couplet, but they all agree in a
geographical way. It was the same with that dreamy teacher-poet,
John Wilson, who wrote in 1764 a descriptive poem entitled "The
Clyde" and gave this account of the source:

From one vast mountain bursting on the day,
Tweed, Clyde and Annan urge their separate way.

> To Anglia's shores bright Tweed and Annan run,
> That seeks the rising, this the setting sun.

But the poet goes on to describe scenes of battle and bloodshed on the Tweed and the Annan and says:

> Clyde far from scenes of strife and horror fled
> And through more peaceful fields his waters led.

It was this John Wilson, by the way, who was offered the mastership of Greenock Grammar School on condition that he should abandon "the profane and unprofitable art of poetry making". Poor John needed the money, and so he gave up poetry. From 1767, when he became headmaster in Greenock, he never wrote another line of verse, as far as anyone knows. Today he is remembered only for "The Clyde".

The eighteenth-century savants were quite satisfied that the Clyde rose near Beattock Summit. The Rev. James Maconochie wrote an account of Crawford parish in 1792 and stated categorically that "the three principal rivers in the south of Scotland, viz. the Clyde, the Tweed and the Annan have their sources in the hills which divide us from Tweedsmuir". This, to a certain extent, is true, because the real source of the Clyde, the Daer Water, does have its source in the same Lowther Hills, but on the other side altogether from the Tweed and the Annan.

In the nineteenth century geographers took an interest in the River Clyde, and doubts were cast on the traditional source of the Little Clyde Burn. Some of the new authorities said the source was the Powtrail Burn, which came down by Durisdeer from the Dalveen Pass. Others said it was the Daer Water, 2,000 feet up in the Lowther Hills. But romantic writers and local people refused to accept that. They liked the idea that three Scottish rivers should have a similar source, and they rejected all rivals to the Little Clyde.

When Neil Munro, novelist, journalist and romantic, wrote his book, *The Clyde*, in 1907, he admitted that there were some arguments about the source, but he accepted the Little Clyde Burn because it was much easier to get to than any of the others!

Astride the stripling Clyde—otherwise, the Daer Water in the Lowther Hills

T. C. F. Brotchie followed Neil Munro in 1914 with *Glasgow Rivers and Streams*, and he wrote:

A cynical and doubting age has refused to accept the evidence of tradition or poets, and statistical writers and the inquisitorial chroniclers of today have adduced well-defined rules and regulations to prove their predecessors in the wrong. The poetry of folk-memory makes but slender appeal to the iconoclast. The glorious fraternity of wayfarers needs pay scant heed to the growlings of these mental berserkers. Squabbles of the pragmatic precisions are a poor exchange for the romance and legend which form our richest inheritance from the vanished past. Let us seek the birthplace of the Clyde, and let us find it on the shoulder of the hill of the three streams.

Ah, yes, they were the romantic boys in those days! But even Mr. Brotchie had his doubts. He followed the Little Clyde Burn up to Little Clyde Farm, built beside a Roman camp on the famous Watling Street. He was impressed by the fact that the farmer of Little Clyde was a Mr. Thomson, who was a descendant of Sergeant-Major Ewart, the hero of the celebrated fight for the French standard at Waterloo. Ewart was a shepherd at a farm called Biddies not far away from Little Clyde.

The Little Clyde Burn starts as a spring some way up from the farm and runs under the railway line. Neil Munro took this way too, and his story was that his walking companion wondered what would happen if he stuck a cork in the tiny outlet of the spring. According to Munro, he did just that, and the two of them decided to see the result. They envisaged ships lying high and dry all the way from Glasgow harbour to the Firth. But when they got back to Glasgow, they found the river flowing just as usual. Neil Munro, of course, was a great man for inventing stories that *could* be true.

I have said that T. C. F. Brotchie had his doubts about the source. He spent some time around Little Clyde Farm and met a local man who told him that the Little Clyde Burn was not the true source of the river. He pointed out a burn which came down the next glen to the south and said that, until the railway came along, this was known as the Little Clyde. It flowed west and

2

Underneath the man-made Daer Dam lie farms and crofts on the old road to the source of the Clyde

joined the Daer Water above Elvanfoot. But it interfered with the line of the railway, and the engineers diverted its course, so that it now flowed south and joined the Evan Water.

I mention all these conjectures about the source of the Clyde because people are conjecturing even yet. When I walked the whole length of the river in 1941 and ended up at the source of the Daer Water, indignant natives of Lanarkshire wrote letters to the Editor saying that I was completely wrong. Modern geographers have no doubt at all that the source of a river, if it is early joined by various streams, is the longest tributary, and the Daer Water is quite easily that.

The people who live up the Daer Valley feel that the whole river should be known not as the Clyde but as the Daer (pronounced 'Dahr'). In that case Sir Harry Lauder's famous song:

> Roamin' in the gloamin'
>   On the bonny banks o' Clyde,
> Roamin' in the gloamin'
>   Wi' a lassie by your side

should be rewritten as:

> Roamin' in the gloamin'
>   On the bonny banks o' Daer,
> Roamin' in the gloamin'
>   Wi' a lassie in your car!

Nowadays the Daer is not only the source of the Clyde. It is the source of a water supply for a large part of Lanarkshire. Half way up the Daer Valley a great dam has been built, and there is now an artificial loch with its surface hundreds of feet above the road, the farms and the crofts which I saw in 1941 and even in 1950.

I walked up to the source of the Clyde from Watermeetings where the Daer joins the Powtrail. At Watermeetings House the celebrated actor, Wilson Barrett, lived for a while. His most famous play was *The Sign of the Cross*, and, appropriately, he is commemorated in a stained glass window in Elvanfoot Church not far away. John Masefield also stayed at Watermeetings and wrote there. Not far up the Daer Road is the farm of Nunnerie, where a Scottish poet, Bessie J. B. MacArthur, lived for many years.

The Daer names are a poem in themselves—Nunnerie, Watermeetings, Hitteril, Hapturnell, Nether Sweetshaw, Upper Sweetshaw and Kirkhope, to name a few. But some of these names exist no more because they are at the bottom of the dam.

The road up to the dam is a good one, naturally. In 1940 it was a road and no more. A school bus went up from Elvanfoot every working day and a few farmers had cars. Otherwise everybody walked. Daer School, the last school in Lanarkshire, is 1,000 feet up in the hills. When I saw it first it consisted of a single room and a house alongside, in which the teacher, Miss Marlinn, lived. She was small and stout and much beloved by her score or so of pupils. She was also famous locally for having been arrested as a spy in Turkey during the Great War. Anyone less like Mata Hari would be hard to imagine.

Nowadays Daer School has been considerably extended. All round the ramparts of the dam there are new houses and lots of children. What was once a lonely little school in the wilds is now a community centre.

My two walks to the source of the Clyde were arduous but delightful, even if it poured all day in 1941. Each time I came to a bridge I took a note that this must be the first bridge over the Clyde. But there always seemed to be one higher up. At last I came to Daerhead, a shepherd's croft which is the last inhabited place in Lanarkshire. I was following the Daer still, but now it was so narrow that I could jump across it easily. At one point I decided to cross to the other side and put my foot on a slippy stone in the middle of the burn. I fell in and sat solidly in the Daer. But I was already so wet that I just sat there and laughed.

(It was not until next day that I discovered I had staved the index finger of my right hand. It wasn't in the least painful, but even today there is nearly half an inch of difference in the length of the index finger of my right and left hands. I can't bend the right finger properly but, when I was having my medical examination for the army in the last war, a doctor had a look at it and said, "Oh, yes, you can pull a trigger all right!")

I got out of my seat in the burn and staggered ever upwards. Then I faced a problem. The Daer (or Clyde) was a mere trickle by this time. But here and there it was joined by another trickle. I had to decide for myself which was the main trickle. But eventually I followed the last of my trickles to a damp green patch in the heather. When I moved some of the undergrowth aside, I saw the spring bubbling up steadily. The rain poured down. I couldn't see the tops of the Lowther Hills for mist. Here and there a wet sheep moved and sometimes coughed.

But I felt exalted. I thought of the great River Clyde, which meant so much to the world and me. To the world, because a global war had started and the Clyde had a big part to play in it. To me, because I was born on its shores and had an atavistic love for the river. It seemed odd to watch the little bubbles coming up in that green patch and think of their end in the Firth of Clyde, that indescribably beautiful entrance to the Atlantic.

I slithered back down the burn to Daerhead, and there the shepherd's wife gave me tea and homemade scones and paid no attention at all to the fact that the water pouring off me had formed a pool round my feet. What she wanted to know was when my newspaper articles on the safari would appear, so that she could send them to her sister in Biggleswade, or some such outlandish place.

As I have said, I walked to the source of the Clyde again in 1950. But this time the chief engineer in charge of the building of the dam gave me a lift from Crawford up to the dam workings. (This didn't invalidate my claim to be walking the whole length of the Clyde from the Broomielaw to the source, since I had to walk all the way back to Crawford. I didn't see much sense in covering part of the distance twice.) The result was that I hadn't the chance to call in at the school and see if my old friend, the Turkish spy, was still teaching there.

But already the houses were growing and the school was extending. I wondered if now I'd have the same strange experience that I had in Miss Marlinn's day. She had introduced me to the school children as someone from Glasgow, where the Daer Water eventually reached. I asked the children how many of them had been in Glasgow, and two boys put up their hands. When I tried to describe how the Daer turned into the Clyde and the wonders that lay along its banks, I could see that they simply did not understand me. The remote Daer Valley was the world to them, and if they'd seen the Daer join the other burns and become the Clyde near Crawford, that was as far as they wanted to go.

In 1951, I imagine, I'd have quite different replies from the school children, whose families had come up from the industrial belt to work on the Daer dam. The Daer itself was still running free. The great rampart was growing across the face of the glen, but otherwise Hitteril and Hapturnell and the rest of them were much the same as I had seen them nine years before. This time, though, I was trying to imagine the time when the dam was closed and the water rose and this very road on which I was walking would be far under water. I came to little houses which were already deserted and, though the day was as fine as the last one had been foul, I shivered as I walked up to Daerhead.

When I got to the shepherd's croft, I found that the people I had met in 1941 were gone. The new shepherd was just going out to see after his flock, and he took me up the little Daer Water to a wall. Then he cut off over the hills. At this point the Daer runs through a cutting in the wall. I climbed over and started up the burn. Soon I found that I was having the same difficulties that I'd experienced nine years before. When it came to trickles, which was the biggest trickle?

In 1941 it was pouring. Now it was a lovely sunny day. I presume that made a difference because I tracked the source of the Clyde down to a different place. This time, instead of a green patch where the undergrowth had to be pulled aside to see the spring bubbles coming up, there was an open spring on a bed of gravel. How different from the River Thames, where the source is so apparent that a plaque is placed at it to tell you that here starts the River Thames.

No wonder Dr. George Pratt Insh has called the Clyde the elusive river. Even in its source, or sources, it is elusive. The Duke of Buccleuch owns all the ground round Daerhead, but I doubt if even he knows the actual source of the river. Perhaps nowadays we should regard the Daer dam as the beginning of the Clyde. There's certainly no mistaking it.

I went up there by car not long ago (and felt sorry I wasn't walking instead!). The Daer Water, on the way up from Nunnerie, looked a little diminished but still a good-going burn. In any case, the Daer has been famous since history began for sudden and heavy floods.

There was, as I have said, a new village round the dam itself. Other evidence of man's handiwork was on the top of the Lower Hills—the three towers of a radio station run by the Ministry of Civil Aviation. The man-made loch looked fine, though I couldn't help thinking of Hitteril and Hapturnell underneath, to say nothing of Nether and Upper Sweetshaw. There was a fair road round one side of the loch, and we took it to a small bridge over a vestigial burn, still the Daer Water and the ultimate Clyde. Across the bridge the track to Daerhead went on. I wondered if I should go up it and have a third look for the source of the Clyde.

But then, I reflected, I might find yet another source. Geographers make things difficult. If they'd just left the source of the Clyde as the spring which starts the Little Clyde Burn, we wouldn't have any doubts. Or would we?

CHAPTER III

THE RIVER ROBERT BURNS KNEW

Soon after Watermeetings the Little Clyde Burn joins the combined Daer and Powtrail Waters, and there is no longer any argument about sources or names. The combined waters are called the River Clyde, and it remains so for the rest of its way to the sea. It is set in a crescent of hills which mark the boundary between the countries of Lanarkshire and Dumfriesshire—or Clydesdale and Nithsdale, as river-loving people have it.

This crescent of hills has several glens. I have dealt already with the Daer glen. The Powtrail comes down the Dalveen Pass by the village of Durisdeer to join the Daer at Watermeetings. Durisdeer Church is worth visiting to see the Durisdeer Marble. The second Duke of Queensberry was King William's Commissioner to the Parliament of Scotland in Edinburgh in 1701, before the Parliaments of Scotland and England were combined.

The Duke was deeply in love with his wife, and when the Duchess died in London in 1709, he brought her remains to Durisdeer and in the kirk he put up a tablet with this inscription, "To his matchless wife, James, Duke of Queensberry and Dover, has caused this monument to be erected with this hope and only solace, that in the same tomb where he has placed these beloved ashes he will place his own."

He died just two years later, and his hope and solace were realized. Now above the graves are the marble effigies of the Duke and Duchess of Queensberry.

The Dalveen Pass is one way down to the Clyde. Another is the Enterkin Pass on Loudon Hill. Here the Covenanters fought against Claverhouse's dragoons in July 1684 and won. All this part of Scotland was strong for the Covenant, and many Covenanters and Cameronians hid in these hills and held their conventicles in secret places, with sentries posted to give warning to the worshippers if the Government troops were seen.

It's not so far from this part of the River Clyde to Douglas, the village where the Cameronians were raised by Richard Cameron, a fighting preacher who defied the dragoons for many years. At last he was captured and killed. The dragoons cut off his head and his hands and brought them into an inn at Douglas to show that he was indeed dead. This had exactly the opposite effect from what they intended. The people of the district adhered all the more to the Covenant, and from them the regiment of Cameronians was raised, a Scottish rifle regiment which had a great history until the War Office killed it, with others, in recent years.

When the Cameronians went to church parade, they posted armed sentries round the church, in the same way that the Covenanters had done all these years before. During the last war the Cameronians had a battalion that was almost entirely Roman Catholic. When this battalion went to church parade, they posted sentries round the Roman Catholic church just as if they were staunch Presbyterians waiting for an attack! On the very last day of its existence, the regiment held a conventicle at Douglas and posted their armed sentries for the last time.

But I must return to the crescent of hills round the infant Clyde. It is completed by the highest villages in Scotland, Wanlockhead and Leadhills. Wanlockhead is slightly higher than Leadhills, and the road from Elvanfoot runs up to both of these clachans. This area, particularly Crawford Muir, was called "God's Treasure House in Scotland". As you can guess from the name, Leadhills was the place where lead was mined. But gold and silver were also found hereabouts, and there were great safaris of gold-seekers to this airt in the sixteenth and seventeenth centuries.

Wanlockhead is a quiet wee place nowadays, but here the first lending library in Scotland is said to have been founded. One of its inhabitants was Allan Ramsay, the author of the play, *The Gentle Shepherd*, revived at least once for the Edinburgh

International Festival of the Arts. Allan has a statue to himself in Princes Street, Edinburgh, today.

One of the first steamships in the world was sailed here—on Dalswinton Loch by the local inventor, Symington. Some people claim that it was the first practical steamship ever made, but one has to be careful when claiming records. Henry Bell of Helensburgh gets the credit in Glasgow of putting the first practical steamer on the Clyde in 1812. But nearly twenty years before that Symington sailed his steamboat on the local loch. One of the impressed passengers was Scotland's national poet, Robert Burns.

Burns knew this part of Scotland and the River Clyde very well. As a farmer, a poet (a successful poet with money in his pocket!), and later as an exciseman, he roamed up and down the river. Much of the Clyde today is as he saw it. Once the main road south to Carlisle ran close to the Clyde, but now the motorway bypasses both Elvanfoot and Crawford and the river is left to its elusive self.

Down from the hills comes the Elvan Water, yet another Clyde tributary, and it joins the parent river at Elvanfoot. I have mentioned Elvanfoot, and its kirk with the stained-glass tribute to Wilson Barrett, already. It's as quiet a little place as you'll find on the Clyde. There is a bridge built by Telford, but it has been closed to the public these many years.

The railway to England was important here, and by its side you may see a memorial stone marking the graveyard of a number of Irish labourers who were working on the railroad when a typhoid epidemic overtook them. In my own experience, Elvanfoot Station (no longer in use) was famous because of the pigeon-racing fraternity.

Racing pigeons are known as 'doos' in Scotland, and they have to be trained for such international events as the Rennes race between Belgium and Scotland by taking them to increasingly distant places and releasing them to find their way back to the doocotes.

Once, years ago, I went on the 'doo train' from Coatbridge to Elvanfoot. This train existed for no other purpose than to liberate homing pigeons at various stations. It certainly paid its way in those days, but this, of course, was before so many of the doo fanciers had their own cars. At Coatbridge basket after basket of cooing pigeons was loaded into the vans. Each was carefully labelled as to when the birds should be released. The railwaymen in charge were all doo experts. At various points other baskets were put aboard the doo train.

The young birds, still learning, were liberated at selected stations on the way south. But the first big liberation was at Crawford, which follows Elvanfoot down the Clyde. Most of the doos, however, went on to Elvanfoot, where the train was shunted into a special siding. And here the railwaymen unloosened the baskets. I saw hundreds of birds fly straight up into the air. Against the blue sky they showed first black and then white, and looked sometimes like a giant shower of confetti. Then they started to 'home'. A great group of pigeons would fly round and round together and then, without any apparent signal, they would wing their way north.

You can still see doos being released at various points along the River Clyde. But now there is no doo train. The doo men have their cars. They load their baskets and, here and there along the paths and roads near the river, you'll see them let the birds loose.

You can now walk comparatively quietly along the road from Elvanfoot to Crawford. At one time, as I have indicated, it was the main road south. Crawford, a long straggling village, was known for its hotels and its 'caffs' for long-distance lorry drivers. Now it's known best to fishermen. The Clyde has always been a great fishing river, and at one time, as we'll come to later, Glasgow was famous for its salmon. But industrial developments lower down the river spoiled the fishing, and it's in these upper waters that the good angling lies.

Along the Clyde from Crawford lies Abington, and just outside that village there is a monument in the middle of a field. If you are curious enough to get over a fence and walk to it, you'll find that it is dedicated

In honour of Matthew McKendrick, 1848—1926, Postmaster,

Abington. A worthy man and a fine fisher, he did much to improve angling in all Clydesdale.

> Fish fair an' free
> An' spare the wee anes.

But we are still at Crawford which, most people have difficulty in believing, is actually 800 feet above sea level. The village was a real centre once upon a time, and the Great Crawford Fair was spoken of with awe.

Across the Clyde from Crawford you will see Tower Lindsay, an ancient seat of the Earls of Crawford. It is now officially a 'dangerous ruin'. King James II of Scotland visited Tower Lindsay and invited a number of noble guests to dinner. He said they should "partake of the fruit of the country". When the guests took their places, they found in front of each of them a plate with a cover over it. Grace was said and the guests lifted the covers. Each plate was heaped with silver from the mines of Leadhills.

The Clyde winds quietly from Crawford to Abington and Roberton. There is a road on the east bank, but it is not much more than a farm track—or, at least, that's what it looked like the last time I took it. Even on the rural Clyde things can change quite rapidly. Over on the western side you can see the main road south, with a never-ending line of traffic going down to England and north to Scotland.

Abington, like Crawford, was once on the main road. Now the motorway bypasses it, and it's all the better a village for that. There's a good hotel (but, of course, there are good hotels all the way along the Clyde) and a pleasant road down to the river, which now runs by trees instead of bare banks and looks that much more picturesque. Fishermen, however, would not agree with me.

From Abington onwards the Clyde scene is dominated by Tinto Hill. Dr. George Pratt Insh, not notably given to hyperbole, called Tinto "a Sphinx brooding over Clydesdale". The river circles round Tinto and, somehow or other, the hill has a strange hypnotic effect on most people. Tinto has twin peaks, joined by a ridge, and is 2,335 feet high. It's quite easy to climb it from Symington. In Druid days it was known as 'The Hill of Fire', and there are still all sorts of tales and verses about it.

The late James Bridie invented a Christmas show for Glasgow Citizens' Theatre for the season 1949–50 and he called it *The Tintock Cup*. Bridie (Dr. Osborne H. Mavor in private life) was not only one of Britain's best-known playwrights, he was also an amateur of the traditional Glasgow comic theatre. The Citizens' Theatre had taken over the Royal Princess's Theatre in the Gorbals—they are still there at the time of writing—and Bridie knew that the great Princess's pantomime had a tradition of being exactly thirteen letters long, hence *The Tintock Cup*.

It's got little to do with the River Clyde, but I can't forbear to point out that the Royal Princess's Theatre in Glasgow held the world record for long pantomime runs. The late Jerry Desmonde used to say it was the only pantomime he'd appeared in where you started the season wearing a fur coat and ended it by wearing a straw hat!

Bridie's pantomime, *The Tintock Cup*, was based on an old Lanarkshire rhyme, well known in the Clyde area, which started:

> On Tintock tap there is a mist
> And in that mist there is a kist,
> And in the kist there is a cup. . . .

I won't go through the whole verse, but the burden of it is that on the top of Tinto Hill you'll find a chest hidden by a mist. In this chest is a magic cup. If you drink from the cup, your wish will come true. Bridie's hero and heroine climbed the hill and drank from the cup, and the rest of the pantomime showed their marvellous adventures.

Can the Druids who made Tinto their home have carried out primitive marriage ceremonies here? We know practically nothing about the Druids in this part of Scotland, but ancient traditions persist, and another set of verses includes the lines:

> But tho' a lass were ere so black,
> Let her hae a penny siller,

Set her up on Tinto tap,
The wind will blaw a man till her.

"Black" in this case means plain of face, "penny siller" is a decent dowry, and the last line is easily translated as "The wind will blow a man to her".

Many people who climb to the top of Tinto confess that they feel an unusual atmosphere about the summit. This, of course, is not uncommon in hill and mountain climbing. And if you have been fed on local legend beforehand, it's all the more likely that you will hypnotize yourself into thinking there is something peculiar in the ambience. Perhaps it was this that led my early school-teachers to tell me that the Clyde rose from Tinto.

If the mist is not concealing the kist on Tintock tap, the view is breath-taking. From Tinto summit (where there was a view indicator the last time I was there, but there's vandalism even in this part of Scotland) you can see sixteen counties. You can look north to the Grampians, east to the Bass Rock in the Firth of Forth, west to Goatfell, the mountain on the Isle of Arran in the Firth of Clyde, and south you can see from Cumberland to Ireland. On a really good day you see the Mountains of Mourne.

In the twelfth century three brothers lived round the base of Tinto Hill. They were powerful men, and they started their own settlements. Their names were Robert, Wice or Wicens and Lambkin. Today their settlements are villages along the Clyde—Roberton, Wiston and Lamington. That, at any rate, is the story told by Neil Munro. A different aspect is put upon the scene by George Eyre-Todd, the historian of Glasgow. He says that these names, plus Tancred (hence Thankerton), were those of Norman settlers planted in the region about the time of King David I of Scotland, the monarch who was a "sair sanct for the croon". In other words, King David was an extremely pious man and was wont to put his own wealth, and as much of the wealth of Scotland as he could get hold of, into building churches and abbeys and settling the kind of people he thought would have a good Christian influence over his subjects.

He gave the Normans land, each built a home, and round

that home a village grew. They may have been considerable settlements in the days of Robert, Wice, Lambkin and Tancred, but Roberton, Wiston, Lamington and Thankerton are all very small places today. They stand at various points along the River Clyde between Abington and Carstairs, and it is obvious that the winding river, which keeps turning in upon itself, has changed course several times over the years, which means that here and there a village which was built upon the river is now a considerable distance from it.

From Abington to Lamington the way along the Clyde is fairly clear. But soon after Lamington it becomes Pratt Insh's "elusive river" once again. It is possible, as I have proved for myself, to keep to the banks of the river all this way, but such a journey entails jumping or wading through small tributaries of the Clyde, climbing fences (some of them barbed wire), negotiating small but steep cliffs, and worrying about bulls. All this can be quite a wearing experience and, unless you are determined to see the Clyde at close quarters, you are better to take the nearest road and admire it from afar. Unless, of course, you are an angler, when you will join the assiduous brotherhood along the banks.

I recommend the Lamington road myself, if you want to keep in some touch with the Clyde. From Abington you can also take the road to Roberton, but the river gets farther and farther away, until you are coming into Lanark at Hyndford Bridge, when it suddenly doubles back upon itself and runs below you. This route cuts out a lot of travelling, but it also cuts out a lot of the River Clyde.

Lamington is a charming little village, in which the new is married to the old in a fairly painless way. Old Lamington is very old indeed, but the general layout of the present village was made by Lord Lamington last century. In Lamington House relics of the great Scottish patriot, Sir William Wallace, are preserved, including his chair. Wallace was the man who started the Scottish War of Independence against the English King, Edward I. He was more of a guerrilla fighter than a man for set battles, though he won several notable victories.

Eventually he was betrayed to the English and a mockery of a trial was staged at Westminster. Though he had never sworn allegiance to the English Crown, Wallace was adjudged a traitor and was hanged, drawn and quartered in London.

This barbarity had the opposite effect of what Edward I intended. Robert the Bruce followed in the patriotic footsteps of Wallace and, at Bannockburn in 1314, his Scottish army completely routed the far stronger English army brought north by Edward II, who escaped capture by the skin of his teeth.

The connection of Wallace with Lamington is that, in the ruined Lamington Tower, not far from the present mansion, Marion Bradfute, who was to become Wallace's wife, was born. The time was to come when the English governor of Lanark murdered Wallace's wife, and Wallace extracted a terrible vengeance and went on to lead Scotland some way, at least, to independence.

Another ruin, not so far from Lamington House, is the picturesquely named Bower of Wandell, surrounded on three sides by the Clyde. This was a hunting seat for King James V of Scotland. But it was also the place where he kept his favourite quarry, if I may put it that way. She was Marjory Weir, known as 'The Flower of Nethan'.

Robert Burns was in Lamington in his day, and went to the old church there. Something must have gone far wrong that Sunday, because later the poet wrote an epigram, one of the satirical verses for which he was famous, entitled "The Kirk of Lamington". It read:

> As cauld a wind as ever blew,
> A caulder kirk, and in't but few;
> As cauld a minister's e'er spak,
> Ye'se a' be het ere I come back.

It has been suggested to me that this needs translation into English, which I doubt. However, in case anyone doesn't fully understand the epigram, here it is Anglified:

> As cold a wind as ever blew,
> A colder church, and in it but few;

As cold a minister has ever spoken,
You'll all be hot ere I return.

It doesn't sound so scornful in English, but what some people call Broad Scots, others the Doric, and still others the Lallans, seldom translates well.

Whatever Burns thought of it, Lamington Church is highly regarded by visitors today. They wander about the old kirkyard and read the ancient inscriptions on the tombstones. They admire the fine Norman doorway, and goggle at the jougs and the stool of repentance, which are on show to remind us of the Bad Old Days. The jougs were the Scottish kirk's equivalent of clapping a man in irons. The stool of repentance was one on which a man or woman stood or sat while the minister in the pulpit thundered forth a diatribe on his or her sins. Once, in another church, Robert Burns had to occupy the stool of repentance while a minister denounced him as a vile seducer. It could have been seeing the stool of repentance in the old grey kirk at Lamington that inspired him to his sarcastic lines.

Lamington is such a pleasant place that it's difficult to see why it should inspire ridicule or sarcasm. Yet there is a famous story in the west of Scotland of how the minister of Lamington, years ago, had arranged to preach in Inchinnan near the banks of the River Cart. The Cart is a tributary of the Clyde and, since the Clyde is tidal at this point, is tidal too. But you can imagine that someone coming from Lamington and seeing the river there would perhaps not know about tides.

At any rate, T. C. F. Brotchie tells the story of

the minister of Lamington who, accompanied by his faithful minister's man, had journeyed on horseback from the lonely upland parish to assist his brother of Inchinnan. As the couple forded the waters (of the Cart) at Inchinnan, they admired the modest stream that wimpled over a pebbly bed.

On the fine Sabbath morn the beadle was early astir, doubtless to sharpen his wits for sermon tasting, of which he was a noted expert, although profoundly ignorant of the law of tides. Strolling down to the river, he was amazed to see the waters rushing in the opposite

Bonnington Falls, near Lanark, seldom seen like this nowadays unless after heavy rain

direction to what he had last seen them. A terrible fear gripped his heart. The 'day of judgment' had arrived, and the waters were hastening to deluge the land.

The poor man fled to the manse, awakened the minister, and in awe-struck tone related the awful news. The minister promptly reminded his horror-struck follower that the last judgment was to be by fire, and then turned, and resumed his nap, while the appeal to The Word, let us hope, calmed the fears of the 'man'.

This is a typically 'Scotch' story of some sixty years ago. It may well be true, and there may be something about Lamington which I can't see, that lends itself to this kind of tale.

I have chosen to follow the Clyde from the Lamington road. Across the river you can see the villages of Roberton and Wiston, but you will find the walking or the driving quieter on this side. You will also find Lamington and the scattered little clachan of Coulter more picturesque than the places across the Clyde. Don't worry, by the way, about the different spellings of some of these names. Wiston can appear as Whiston and Coulter as Culter. It's an old Scottish custom to have at least a couple of spellings of every place name.

The Clyde is still very much a fishing river hereabouts. You come to a main road from Coulter where the way to Biggar runs to the right and to Symington to the left. Once again, unless you are actually following the River Clyde on its banks, you must make a decision. You can go by Biggar, Liberton, Carnwath and Carstairs and see the elusive Clyde only occasionally until you turn south again to Hyndford Bridge. Or you can go direct to Hyndford Bridge by way of Symington and Thankerton, and still see the elusive Clyde only occasionally. Between these two roads the river runs north and then makes a great sweep round to the west. Once again the scenery appeals mainly to fishermen.

If you decide to go right you come very soon to the pleasant little country town of Biggar, a place which, as we say in Scotland, has a good conceit of itself. The local people will tell you pawkily, "Aye, London's big, but Biggar's Biggar!" (This sounds better than it reads.) It has the wide main street that is typical of towns in the south of Scotland, and some good shops and hotels.

3

Cora Linn in flood

Cora Linn in the winter of 1895

Indeed, it is quite a tourist resort, especially since it's on the main road to Edinburgh.

The old kirk of Biggar dates from the Middle Ages. In the kirkyard are the unmarked graves of the farmer ancestors of William Ewart Gladstone, once Prime Minister of Britain. Biggar was also the birthplace of a much esteemed Scottish author, Dr. John Brown, who wrote a widely-read book about dogs (and human beings) entitled *Rab and His Friends.*

The only other antiquity around Biggar is the ruin of Boghall Castle. Edward II of England slept here, when he was trying to cow the rebellious Scots in vain. And Mary Queen of Scots stayed here briefly in 1565. But, if you are lucky, you may see another sign of olden days. Once a year the Royal Company of Archers, the Queen's Bodyguard in Scotland, go to Biggar to shoot for the Silver Arrow. In their magnificent green and black uniforms, with feathers shooting from their swirling bonnets, they march through the town headed by their pipe band to the place where the targets are set up. They are real archers, by the way, and can hold their own in contests with such rivals as the Bowmen of Sherwood Forest.

The field where the Archers draw their long bows was known for rather sterner military affairs during World War Two. The Polish Army, or at least that part of it which escaped from France at the time of Dunkirk and after, was reconstituted in the south-west of Scotland, mainly at Biggar and nearby. I recall seeing a great parade of Polish soldiers before General Sikorski at Biggar, where the Glasgow Police Pipe Band distinguished themselves by playing the Polish National Anthem on the bagpipes. General Sikorski recognized the tune too!

The Biggar accent is a strong Scottish Lowland one, and many of the Poles thought they were speaking English when they were actually speaking Scots. It was only when they moved out of the area, and especially into England, that they found their 'English' was not understood. Indeed, some people in the south thought they were still speaking Polish.

A side road leads from Biggar to Carnwath and Carstairs. It runs by the little clachan of Liberton, which is as close as you can get to the Clyde on either side of the river. Carnwath is one of the typical straggling villages of this region and is strangely mixed between the very old and the very new. It stands on the Carnwath Burn, a tributary of the Clyde. The old church, with its College Aisle, is worth seeing, and there are the vestigial ruins of Couthally Castle, once a seat of the Somervilles.

Once a year there is the Carnwath Fair and Games, at which a very ancient foot race is run for the Carnwath Red Hose. These red stockings are knitted each year by Carnwath women, and a pair of them is the prize for the race. Winning the Red Hose race is considered a great honour, and there are usually plenty of runners.

From Carnwath it's a short journey to Carstairs, partly an old village and partly a railway junction. It is the parting of the lines from the south to Edinburgh and Glasgow. A well-known Scottish comedienne, Jean Kennedy, used to say to her audience, "I've as many lines on ma face as Carstairs Junction!" and it always got a laugh. The old village, however, lies on the Roman road called Watling Street, and there are still traces of the Roman occupation at Castledykes. To get to the Clyde from Carstairs you must now go south, to Hyndford Bridge. The way round from Biggar by Carnwath and Carstairs is nearly twice as long as the road you can take to the left after passing Coulter.

If you choose the left road you soon come on a high bridge crossing the Clyde. The road leads up to Symington, a pretty little village which is known as the best place to start climbing Tinto Hill and for its Tinto Hotel. This hotel looks rather foreign to the countryside, and that may be because it was founded by one François Imhoff, well known in Glasgow as a member of the Bridgeton Burns Club (the largest Burns club in the world) and on the east coast of the country for holing a shot in one at Cockermouth Golf Course.

Past Symington you join the road north from Abington and Roberton and circle Tinto Hill to Thankerton, where, once again, you are near the Clyde. Here you see the conical hill named Quothquhan, which seems to me, every time I look at it, to have some of the magic of Tinto, though it's so much smaller. Perhaps it's the queer name which has this effect, but I feel that almost anything might happen if you spent a night on Quothquhan.

From Thankerton it's not long to Hyndford Bridge, built in 1773. At last you are at the elusive river once more. The Clyde is flowing below the bridge. But you still have problems. Once again the river runs south and, if you are very determined, you can follow it. But you will be faced by the Douglas Water, a considerable tributary and not easy to cross.

When I walked this way I found I had to make a very wide detour to get from Hyndford Bridge to the west bank of the Clyde. It involved going as far as Douglas Mill and tramping through farmer's fields for what seemed miles. The easy way, and the way which I counsel, is to go straight across the bridge and up the hill to Lanark. From Lanark, as I shall demonstrate in the next chapter, you can go to possibly the most romantic and beautiful parts of the whole River Clyde.

CHAPTER IV

THE FALLS OF CLYDE

From the point at which the often turbulent Daer Water joins the other tributaries, the Clyde is not a dramatic river. It flows placidly (to the great delight of anglers) in various sweeps round Tinto until it turns back on its tracks at Carstairs and runs under Hyndford Bridge. As I have just said, following the river at this point is difficult—and I must report that it's not worth the trouble.

Take the high road from Hyndford Bridge to Lanark and go back down to the Clyde from that ancient Royal Burgh. You go into Lanark by Winston Barracks, named after the most famous of the Churchills, and by Lanark Racecourse, which may look quite modern to you but claims to have the oldest horse race in Scotland. The Lanark Silver Bell is said to have been given to the town in the year 1100 as a racing trophy by King William the Lion of Scotland. But experts have identified a hallmark on it of the Edinburgh goldsmiths, showing that it really dates from about the end of the sixteenth century.

It must be said, at this point, that there is another claimant to the title of the oldest horse race in Scotland. This is the race for working farmhorses on Marymass Day in the town of Irvine on the Ayrshire coast. The Silver Bell at Lanark is a straightforward race run by trained horses. But the Carters' Race at Irvine is run by huge Clydesdales, which tear round the rugged course, digging great pieces of turf into the air and sometimes unseating their amateur jockeys.

It's impossible to say whether the Lanark or the Irvine race is the older, but Irvine has the advantage of a strong Carters' Society, a secret sodality with a password, a 'grip' and an initiation ceremony still carried out. The Irvine Carters are much more vocal than anyone concerned with the Lanark Silver Bell, and so it has become generally understood that the Marymass Race is the older one.

On the other hand, the people of Lanark can produce their Silver Bell and have racing records going back many years. I write this with a certain amount of feeling, because I was responsible for the questions in a B.B.C. television programme called "Quizburgh", in which various burghs in Scotland competed. One of the questions concerned the oldest horse race in the country, and my answer was the Marymass race at Irvine. Ever since then I have been involved in controversy between Lanark and Irvine, and I have not the slightest doubt that the publication of this book will start it all over again.

From the Lanark racecourse you go in by the cattle market (a very important one in these parts) and reach the broad main street that runs down a hill to the Clyde. Its breadth is brought to a halt by a sudden complex of narrow ways and the old parish church with a statue of Sir William Wallace gazing blankly up the Westport and the High Street. The blank look is misleading. It was in Lanark that Wallace virtually started the Scottish War of Independence, which, as I have said, ended in Robert the Bruce's victory at Bannockburn in 1314.

Wallace was the younger son of Sir Malcolm Wallace of Elderslie, near Paisley and not far from Glasgow. From his schooldays he was an ardent patriot and resented the way that the English army had taken over his part of Scotland. When he was a youth he was fishing in the River Ayr and had a good catch of trout. He was taking the trout home in a basket when an English soldier ordered him to hand it over. A fight started and young Wallace killed the Englishman.

He escaped the vengeance of the army, but he could not stop fishing. He went up the River Clyde for a fishing holiday and, as all good anglers did in the thirteenth century, he went to church on Sunday. The kirk he chose was St. Kentigern's at Lanark. In the congregation he saw the beautiful Marion

Braidfute of Lamington and fell in love with her. Marion fell in love with Wallace, and it was not long ere they were married in the twelfth-century church. Vestigial remains of St. Kentigern's can still be seen today.

By getting married Wallace was landing himself into a ready-made feud. The English garrison at Lanark were quartered in the old castle (you can still visit the Castlehill), where the first Scottish Parliament met under King Kenneth II in the year 978. King Alexander I made Lanark into a royal burgh, and his brother, who became King David I, rebuilt Lanark Castle and lived in it. Now the English garrison lived there, under the command of William de Hesliope or, to the Scots, Hazelrig.

Now Hazelrig wanted his son to marry Marion Braidfute and he was prepared to go to any lengths to achieve a happy wedding. But Marion refused young Hazelrig, and the governor of Lanark laid siege to the Braidfute place at Lamington. Marion's father, Hugh Braidfute, and his son were killed, but Marion escaped. Apparently young Hazelrig was not able to press his suit any further, but father and son were annoyed when William Wallace married the girl.

Wallace and his wife lived in a house in the Castlegate, and the day came when they were visited by Wallace's friend, Sir John Graham. The young husband decided to take his friend out for a walk through Lanark. Wallace was wearing a new green suit, which his wife much admired. As he and Sir John were walking through the town, some English soldiers appeared from an inn and one of them made a sarcastic remark about the bright green of Wallace's suit. Wallace pretended not to hear, but the soldier put out his hand and touched Wallace's sword. This was an unpardonable insult at that time. Wallace drew his sword and killed his second English soldier.

The other soldiers attacked immediately, and they were joined by more men from the garrison. But Wallace and Graham hacked their way through to the Castlegate and escaped into Wallace's house. They then ran from the back door of the house to the wood on Cartland Crag, near where the bridge stands today.

Word of the affray went immediately to the governor, and

Hazelrig rode to the Castlegate with a body of troopers, surrounded Wallace's house, and ordered it to be burned down. Marion Braidfute and three servants were burned alive. It's thought, charitably, that Hazelrig was certain that Wallace and Graham were in the house.

When Wallace was told of his wife's death, he came back into the town by night and rallied two or three dozen Lanark men. They entered the castle without difficulty, and Wallace charged into Hazelrig's bedroom and cut the governor's throat while he was asleep on his feather bed. The garrison were roused, but in their sleepy state they were no match for the men of Lanark. It is said that 240 of them perished that night. And after that Sir William Wallace was a wanted man.

In the Castlegate there is a tablet which says simply—

> Here stood the house of
> William Wallace
> who, in Lanark, in 1297
> first drew sword
> to free his native land.

Wallace's statue on the old parish church at the Westport doesn't seem to me to do him justice. And it looks rather odd once a year, on Lanimer Day, when it is decorated with a floral wreath. Lanimer Day, held early in June, is the climax of 'The Lanimers', a series of ceremonies lasting nearly a week. A Cornet is appointed to represent Lanark, and there is a riding of the marches of the town to see that no usurper is intruding on the common land of the royal burgh.

Lanimer Day brings Lanark expatriates from all over the world. A Lanimer Queen has been elected from one of the town schools, and she is crowned on a high dais just below Wallace's statue. Before this there is a great procession through the town, a procession so big and so finely dressed that if it took place somewhere on the Continent it would be world famous. I have been a judge at Lanimer Day, so I know.

From miles around people flock into Lanark, and the whole route of the procession is packed. Stands are built round the dais where the queen is to be crowned, and round here, naturally, the crowd is thickest. The last time I was there the procession included eleven bands, the Cornet and his mounted followers, the Provost of Lanark with the bailies and councillors, the Lanimer Queen's own procession with knights, heralds, ladies-in-waiting and pages, and one great set piece after another. These set pieces are on an amazing scale for such a small town. I remember one of *Alice in Wonderland* where the main characters posed on a travelling float, surrounded by walking actors and actresses portraying minor characters. They included fifty-two children dressed as every card in the pack.

One part of the procession which always intrigues visitors who have never been to Lanimer Day before is the group of young men and boys carrying birch tree boughs. This is a relic of the time when the lairds round about Lanark tried to encroach on the town. One way to take over ground was to plant trees on it. So the independent Lanarkians would go out and uproot the trees. This independence is commemorated on Lanimer Day, but it must be admitted that every boy who brings a birch bough along receives a reward—formerly a shilling, now fivepence.

When the Lanimer Queen and her retinue have mounted the dais, surrounded by all the gaily-dressed children who have taken part in the procession, the crowd closes in and fills the High Street for as far as one can see. I remember an elderly man, with tears in his eyes, saying to me, "Ye could walk ower their heids!" I don't think anybody would have been allowed to walk over their heads, but I could see what he meant.

There's not quite such a big turn-out for another Lanark tradition which takes place at approximately the same spot. This is an odd rite called 'Whuppity Scoorie', performed in front of the Provost of Lanark by local children during the winter. The children parade with balls of paper tied to string, and at a given signal they run round and round the old kirk, each trying to hit the child ahead of him. As far as anybody knows, this has something to do with a witch who was scourged from Lanark in mediaeval times, but the origins are uncertain. What is certain is that the children, like the birch-bough carriers on Lanimer Day, receive a small fee as appearance money.

The River Clyde is part of the boundary of the town of Lanark, and you can reach it by several routes. Lanark is the county town of Lanarkshire (though Hamilton is the civic centre), and the main road to the industrial part of the county does not touch the Clyde, though it does cross the Mouse Water, a tributary with a ford which is one of the marches of Lanark sought out on Lanimer Day. There are two main ways to the Clyde from the town, and we'll take the one to New Lanark first of all. It is clearly sign-posted and is not much more than a mile long, all downhill, south of Lanark itself. It stands on the Falls of Clyde, but to see these famous falls properly the westerly road to Kirkfieldbank is the better way.

But no one following the Clyde should miss New Lanark and, though it means looking at the river first from one side and then the other, the consequent wide detour is still worth taking.

New Lanark was founded in 1785 by a remarkable Stewarton man named David Dale. He is supposed to have been the person on whom Sir Walter Scott modelled the character of Bailie Nicol Jarvie in *Rob Roy*. You can see his portrait on the Royal Bank of Scotland £5 and £1 notes.

When you go down the steep hill into New Lanark you see the long stone buildings of David Dale's mills and in front of them the model tenements which he built for his workers. Behind these buildings is the Clyde, rolling much faster than you have seen it before because it has come down a series of falls. In ten years David Dale built four mills here, all driven by the River Clyde and giving employment to 1,334 workers. He chose the place originally because it was just below the Dundaff Linn Falls, which look little more than a weir now. Hydro-electric power stations have taken away the grandeur of the Falls of Clyde except in times of unusual rainfall.

David Dale was the son of an Ayrshire grocer. His first job was herding cattle, but as a youth he went to Paisley to serve his apprenticeship as a weaver. When he was twenty-four he went to Glasgow and was soon a wealthy man, importing fine yarns from France and Holland. An English company built the first cotton mill in Scotland at Rothesay on the Isle of Bute in the Firth of Clyde. But it was David Dale who bought it over and developed it.

Business developers think they are mighty fine fellows today, but David Dale could have taught them a thing or three. He liked the look of the Falls of Clyde and so he bought a parcel of land by the river from Macqueen of Braxfield (the Law Lord who was transformed into Weir of Hermiston by R. L. Stevenson). The plantation trade between the Clyde and America had collapsed soon after the outbreak of the American War of Independence, and David Dale was looking for new fields to conquer.

The first Chamber of Commerce in the world was established in New York. The second was established in Glasgow. David Dale was a leading member of the Glasgow Chamber of Commerce, and when the Chamber gave a dinner in honour of Arkwright, the inventor of the spinning jenny, he talked to Arkwright about his land by the Falls of Clyde. A day or two later David Dale took Arkwright out to see the site, and the English inventor was impressed by the place and the power of the river as it came down four falls in succession. They agreed to go into partnership.

David Dale built the first mill at New Lanark in 1785, but soon afterwards the partners were at loggerheads and Arkwright left for England. Dale's biggest problem was to get a sufficient labour force to work his mills. The population of Lanark, on the hill above him, was not capable of providing the labour he needed. He advertised in various newspapers, particularly in Glasgow.

This was the time when many Highlanders and their families were leaving Scotland to seek their fortune in the Americas. One shipful of emigrants was driven by storm into the Firth of Clyde. As they sheltered there the emigrants read the newspapers and saw David Dale's advertisement offering work in the New Lanark cotton mill. The entire boatload decided not to cross the Atlantic but to go up the Clyde to New Lanark. This was David Dale's first group of workers, and it was followed by other parties of Highlanders who were told of the good wages and conditions he offered.

As he kept on extending the New Lanark mills, David Dale needed more and more workers. In those days child labour was not only universally accepted but considered a most desirable thing for the offspring of the lower (one might almost say the lowest) classes. David Dale got his eyes on the poor houses of Glasgow and Edinburgh where there were many children, orphaned or abandoned. He made arrangements to employ them at New Lanark and he gave them not only accommodation and food such as they had never experienced, but also established schools and medical centres. And he built the tenements which, however they may look today, were far ahead of their time in the eighteenth century.

David Dale was a very religious man and taught himself Greek and Hebrew so that he could understand the Bible properly. For thirty-seven years he was pastor of the Greyfriars Wynd Old Scots Independent Church (actually Congregational) in Glasgow. When he started his mills on the Clyde he introduced his religious ideas, and every worker had to attend morning and evening service every day. Since they worked, on an average, twelve hours a day and attended educational classes (including nature study) in the evening, they didn't find time hanging heavy on their hands!

In front of me, as I write, is one of David Dale's 'silent monitors'. One of them hung by every worker in the mills. It is a triangular piece of wood, painted a different colour on each side— black, yellow, and white. It has a hook on the top, so that it can be hung on to the end of a loom. According to which colour faced outwards, the operator and the visitor knew how the operator was progressing. If it was black, the boy or girl was doing badly. Yellow meant that he or she was a passable worker. White—need I say it?—meant that the work was up to David Dale's standard. (My own 'silent monitor', given to me at the New Lanark mills, is showing black at this moment—this manuscript should have been in the hands of my publishers some months ago!)

David Dale's schools, attached to the mills at New Lanark, were regarded as models for their day. On an average 25,000 people visited them every year. The children were taught music and dancing as well as the usual subjects, and they had their own band. When the Russian Grand Duke who became the Czar Nicholas I, visited the schools he was greeted by the New Lanark Band, toured the mills, saw the Falls of Clyde, and was played out by the New Lanark Band at the end of what to them must have been an almost lazy day.

But New Lanark was only part of David Dale's interests. Among many other business and philanthropic activities, he was joint agent in Glasgow of the Royal Bank of Scotland. That is why his portrait appears on their banknotes today. (Perhaps I should explain, by the way, for the benefit of non-Scottish readers, that the three Scottish banks issue their own notes, which are generally regarded as of a higher artistic quality than the Bank of England notes.)

Because of these multifarious activities, he sold the New Lanark Mills to a Manchester company in 1799. The new owners appointed as manager an energetic and enterprising young man named Robert Owen, who had sociological ideas somewhat ahead of his time. In particular, Robert Owen started co-operative trading, and today on the premises of the New Lanark Co-operative shop there is a plaque which states, "Robert Owen in these premises carried out his trading experiment in social reform, 1800–24."

David Dale still took a keen interest in the New Lanark Mills and became friendly with young Robert Owen. He invited the new manager to his home in Charlotte Street, Glasgow, not far from the River Clyde as it flowed through that city. Here Robert Owen met Dale's daughter, Anne Caroline, fell in love and married the girl.

Owen became keener and keener on his sociological reforms and experiments and less interested in running New Lanark. Eventually he and his wife left the Clyde and went to America, where he started an experimental community based on complete co-operation. It has been described as the first attempt at a communistic society. It failed, but the Owens remained in America. Some of their descendants still visit Scotland on holiday and make a pilgrimage to New Lanark.

The mills on the Clyde were used for many years for various purposes. They were bought in 1903 by the Gourock Ropework Company and in recent years were producing canvas and synthetic yarn for net-making and twines. The Gourock Ropework Company, of course, have been famous for making the ropes for the two giant Cunarders, *Queen Mary* and *Queen Elizabeth*, and also for making the big tops used by Bertram Mills' Circus. In 1967, owing to foreign competition, the company had to retrench and closed down two of its factories, one of them being the New Lanark Mills.

The situation has changed completely since then. Part of the mills have been taken over by the Metal Extraction Company. The New Lanark Association is campaigning vigorously for the renewal of the village. There are plans to revive New Lanark at a cost of over £1,000,000 and a company called Scotland Direct has taken over Robert Owen's old Counting House as a centre for the work of Scottish craftsmen.

Across the River Clyde from New Lanark you see the wooded banks of Corehouse Estate, and that is where you must go to see the Falls of Clyde. It means retracing your steps up the steep hill to Lanark—or waiting for the little local bus which keeps up, appropriately, a shuttle service between New Lanark Mills and the royal burgh.

Once back in Lanark, you take the main road to the west, past the Clydesdale Hotel, which is built on the site of one of the religious houses of medieval times in this airt. The wine cellars of the hotel are actually monks' cells, and there is supposed to be a ghostly monk who haunts them, a spirit among the spirits. The ghost has been seen at least once in the last year or so.

To all intents and purposes, Lanark ends at the crossroads, where the main road sweeps round to the industrial part of the county and a road which is even steeper than the New Lanark one runs down to Kirkfieldbank and the River Clyde. Here we are at the beginning of the orchard country of the Clyde, which we'll investigate in our next chapter, along with Kirkfieldbank.

Two bridges cross the Clyde here, the wide new one and the narrow ancient one, now used for foot traffic only. The river here

runs faster and is wider than at any place since the Daer became
the Clyde. True, it seldom runs as fast as in the days when the
Falls of Clyde came down untramelled by a hydro-electric
power scheme. In 1798, for example, a traveller who had come
from Lanark and followed the same way that we are going, could
climb back up the hill to his inn and, before getting into the
coach, write these lines in the inn's guest book—

> What fools are mankind,
> And how strangely inclined,
> To come from all places
> With horses and chaises,
> By day and by dark
> To the falls of Lanark!
> For, good people, after all,
> What is a waterfall?
> It comes roaring and grumbling,
> And leaping and tumbling,
> And hopping and skipping,
> And foaming and dripping,
> And struggling and toiling,
> And bubbling and boiling,
> And beating and jumping,
> And bellowing and thumping.
> I have much more to say upon
> Both Cora Lin [sic] and Bonniton,
> But the trunks are tied on,
> And I must be gone.

Not, maybe, another "How the water comes down at Lodore",
but not bad for an impromptu in the circumstances.

When I went this way last, I climbed up the road which runs
by the hotel to one of the lodges which marks the entrances to
Corehouse estate and took the path through the woods beside the
Clyde. The estate is owned by Colonel Alastair Cranstoun, M.C.,
a descendant of Lord Corehouse, who built Corehouse mansion
near Cora Linn between 1824 and 1827. He has no objections to
visitors to his grounds and, at another entrance, has a notice
directing them to the Falls of Clyde.

I found a group of woodmen cutting down gigantic trees,

some of them across the track I was taking. Some of the biggest trees in Scotland are to be found at Corehouse. Sir Walter Scott and Landseer helped Lord Corehouse to lay out the grounds, although the pride of the estate, the great avenue of beeches, was there long before the author and the artist took to landscaping.

The path led by Corehouse mansion to a wicket gate with a 'Danger' notice beside it. On the other side of that gate the path went on by the steep side of the Clyde. The river was foaming beneath and across on the other side were implacable cliffs. This is no place for anyone with vertigo. Indeed, I would seriously counsel such a person not to go near the Falls of Clyde. It had been raining on the day when I went there and the path was muddy and slippery.

I reached a vantage point where an inadequate looking railing was supposed to prevent visitors from falling down the precipice. I'll admit my knees were shaking. At one time visitors to Cora Linn and Bonniton could take a path on the cliff side of the Clyde and the author of *Law Lyrics*, who took it in 1888, was so impressed that he wrote in *The Falls of Clyde, and other Poems:*

> Back from the edge the astonished pilgrim turns,
> To follow on the winding path, which toils
> Along these cliffs, from whose green edge he sees,
> Through mazy boughs, brief glimpses of the stream,
> The murmur of whose battle rises hoarse
> Into his face whene'er he peeps adown
> The giddy, vast, and leaf-beclouded steep.

Though I was on the other side, and lower down, I felt the same. Perhaps it was even worse for me because, from this vantage point, I had a clear view of the rushing water and not mere "brief glimpses of the stream". I could also see the power station below me to the left.

It was about here that Turner sat and painted his "Falls of Clyde". He included a couple of improbable bathers in the picture. Bathing has been known here but it is not encouraged. One man who is said to have got a wetting here was Sir William Wallace, and a space between two rocks in the middle of the river

Cora Castle, a ruined keep above the Falls of Clyde

is called 'Wallace's Leap'. He was, of course, escaping from the English at the time. Lower down the river, not far from New Lanark, is 'Wallace's Seat', where the hero is supposed to have sat in safety watching his pursuers search in vain.

Across from where I was standing were high cliffs, and I learned later from Colonel Cranstoun that there was a way up them called 'Jacob's Steps'. I felt that the Wallace public relations men had not been doing their work, or it would surely be named 'Wallace's Steps'.

I left my outlook point and went up the track to the small ruin of Cora Castle. Cora Linn and Cora Castle are said to have got their name from the daughter of an ancient king of Scotland. Princess Cora was riding by the falls when her horse took fright. It leapt from the precipice, and horse and princess were swallowed up in the gulf below. I am quoting from *The Scottish Tourist* of 1830, which is as likely to be correct in a legendary way as any other authority.

Cora Castle stands out on a ledge over the falls and is just as vertiginous as the outlook point—perhaps even more so, for it is higher. "Elegy" Gray looked at Cora Linn from this castle, and so, much later, did William Wordsworth, his sister Dorothy and Samuel Taylor Coleridge. They were all impressed by the sight and Coleridge was trying out various adjectives to describe the waterfall. He had discarded grand, majestic, sublime, and a few others, when a stranger looking down from Cora Castle said that it was a "magnificent" waterfall. Dorothy Wordsworth wrote later, "Coleridge was delighted with the accuracy of the epithet."

Wordsworth himself returned to Corehouse mansion and wrote of Cora Linn and Cora Castle:

> Lord of the Vale! astounding flood!
> The dullest leaf in this dark wood
>   Quakes conscious of thy power:
> The caves reply with hollow moan,
> And vibrates to its central stone
>   Yon time-cemented tower.

Today the "time-cemented tower" does not quake so often

4

"Never did stream glide more gracefully to the ocean through a fairer region"

because it's only after very heavy rain that you see it as he and I saw it, some 130 years apart. Incidentally, there is now a notice on the wooden door of the castle saying simply, "Dangerous ruin". It's not so much that Colonel Cranstoun and his right-hand man, Jock Houston, expect to see Cora Castle crumble down the precipice into Cora Linn some day, as that silly young people are apt to try climbing round it. Not long ago Jock Houston had to rescue a young girl who had fallen half way down the less precipitous side and broken her leg.

It was Jock Houston who told me that, even yet, the waterfall can be magnificent, as the man said to Coleridge. In a recent winter so much water came down that the spray from Cora Linn flew over the highest trees and froze into thirty-foot icicles.

Farther up the river is Bonniton Linn, but it is very difficult to reach and in any case is not nearly as spectacular. My own suggestion is that you should be satisfied with Cora Linn. And, indeed, if you are unlucky and there on a day when the water is low, it's simply not worth while making the short but arduous safari to the higher fall. Incidentally, the higher fall is, paradoxically, the lower fall. Cora Linn is nearly three times the height of Bonniton.

CHAPTER V

THE RIVER THAT SCOTT KNEW

Sir Walter Scott drew the inspiration for at least two of his novels from the orchard country of the River Clyde—that is to say, the Clyde from Lanark to Garrion Bridge. It wasn't a great orchard country in his day, although now townspeople in thousands go to this part of the river in May to see the flourish on the fruit trees. But it was an intensely romantic country to Scott—and where it wasn't, like any good writer, he made up the romance!

According to another Scottish novelist and romancer, Neil Munro, Sir Walter was offered part of Craignethan Castle, which we come to on this journey towards Hamilton, as a residence. What if Scott had decided to live here? It might have affected his whole future as a writer. And Craignethan, instead of Abbotsford, would have been a place of pilgrimage for amateurs of Sir Walter all over the world.

As I have said already, Scott was interested in helping to lay out the grounds of Corehouse. He made expeditions from the Falls of Clyde up both banks of the river. On the right bank he got his inspiration for *The Talisman*. Farther up, on the left bank, he drew material from Craignethan for *Old Mortality*.

But, as nice Victorian authors would certainly say, I anticipate. If you are going to follow the River Clyde from Lanark, the better way is by the left bank, through the orchard country, to Hamilton. At first, at Kirkfieldbank, it is plain to be seen. But then it becomes the elusive river once again, winding between high banks, sheltering anglers from the elements, and glimpsed from the roadway only now and again—unless you are prepared to go down narrow lanes or across country to stand upon its banks.

On the right bank the situation is even more difficult. The main road touches the Clyde where the Mouse Water falls down to the river. But after that it goes away from the Clyde by Braidwood, Carluke, Waterloo and Wishaw, through Motherwell to Hamilton and the river banks once more. As I know from my own experience, taking the right bank from Lanark is a series of frustrations. Every now and then you walk hopefully down a track or a farm road, see the Clyde, and then have to walk back the same way to the main highway.

So the pattern of this chapter must be to follow the left bank, and describe the right bank on the appropriate occasions. Accordingly, we have come down the steep hill from Lanark to Kirkfieldbank, a straggling village with a 'modernized' hotel that does not fit into its surroundings, and, on the other side of the Clyde, a beautifully-situated caravan camp. I am no lover of caravan camps, although, like any other reasonable man, I realize their necessity. I know that trailer caravans have revolutionized holidays for many families. But I am old-fashioned enough to regret it when a caravan camp spoils a noted view or makes a mess of what was once a pleasant outlook. Perhaps I should admit that I have no experience whatever of the caravan site opposite Kirkfieldbank. All I can say is that it fits in with the scenery to a remarkable degree.

Kirkfieldbank is a good introduction to the orchard country, for it is a village half way between the town atmosphere of the Royal Burgh of Lanark and the little, fruit-hung clachans along the Clyde. Up behind Kirkfieldbank, towards and beyond Corehouse, there are notable fruit farms, and some of them produce flowers on a big scale as well. At the appropriate time of year you will hear Dutch accents all around this area, for the Dutch bulb and seed growers find a rich harvest here. The visiting Dutchmen live in Lanark hotels, and they have been coming here so often that they now speak English with a Clydeside accent.

The road through Kirkfieldbank hangs over the River Clyde for a spell and then moves above it. Across the river is the entrance of the Mouse Water, which runs down from Cartland Crags and is spanned on the main road by a Telford bridge built in 1822.

Just above the bridge, you may not be surprised to know by now,
is 'Wallace's Cave', on the side of a steep cliff. Some legendary
experts—or should I say experts in legends?—say that this is where
the Scottish hero went after he was pursued by the English
soldiers in Lanark.

The author of *The Scottish Tourist* (1830) puts it like this:

Such is the veneration in which the memory of that illustrious
patriot has been ever held by the peasantry of Scotland, that they
have connected his name, or traditions respecting him, with in-
numerable places supposed to have been dignified with his presence;
but many of these, irregular and desultory as his movements must
have been, it is probable he never visited:

> 'Each rugged rock proclaims great WALLACE' fame,
> Each cavern wild is honour'd with his name;
> *Here* in repose was stretch'd his mighty form,
> And *there* he shelter'd from the night and storm.'

Circumstances, however, tolerably well authenticated, give plausi-
bility to the tradition that Wallace took refuge in this cave.

Cartland Bridge, the Cartland Crags, and the story of Wallace
must have been known to Sir Walter Scott, and it's surprising
that he did not make some literary use of this knowledge. But he
seemed to be captured by the House of Lee, about a mile and a
half along the road from Cartland Bridge, overlooking the Clyde.
Here, for something like 600 years, has been kept the Lee Penny,
which gave Scott the idea for his novel, *The Talisman*.

It is described by John M. Leighton as:

a small, triangular shaped stone, dark red in colour, set in a shilling
of Edward I. It is kept in a gold box with the inscription inside the
lid—"A present from the Empress Queen to General Lockhart, and
given by him to Mrs. Lockhart of Lee, 1789, to hold the Lee-penny."

The story of the Lee Penny goes back to the days of King
Robert the Bruce, the man who followed Sir William Wallace
and achieved independence for Scotland. It was one of Bruce's
ambitions to carry out a knightly crusade. But he had been too

busy fighting for Scotland and ruling the country, and when he was dying he sent for his most famous general, Sir James Douglas, and asked him to take his heart to Jerusalem and deposit it in the Holy Sepulchre.

Douglas was a great warrior. Although he left Scotland in June, 1330, with the most pious intentions, placing his monarch's wish foremost in his heart, he couldn't resist a fight where he found one. Douglas was attended by a great train of Scottish knights and esquires and, while they were going to the Holy Land, they were fully armed for battle. So when he reached Spain and learned that Alphonsus XI, King of Castile and Leon, was waging war on behalf of the Christian Church against the Saracens, he took his army to join the Christian standard.

The Christians met the Saracens in battle at Teva in Andalusia, on the frontiers of Granada. Sir James Douglas led his men into the fight with his customary gusto, but soon found that he was outnumbered by the Saracens. The Spaniards, whether from jealousy or some other reason, had not supported him. When he saw that the battle was going against him, Douglas rose in his stirrups, took the casket containing Bruce's heart from his armour, and threw it far ahead into the host of advancing Saracens, shouting, "Lead on, brave heart, as thou wast ever wont to do!" Then he charged after it and was soon brought down and killed.

After the action was over and the battlefield was deserted, Simon Lockhart of Lee, squire to Sir James Douglas, went out by night and brought back the body of Douglas and the casket containing Bruce's heart. You can see today where Bruce's heart is buried in Melrose Abbey, although his body lies in Dunfermline. The body of Douglas was taken to the place which bears his name and there—as I have said already, not far from the Clyde—you can see in the old Douglas kirk the effigy of the good Sir James, with his heart above it.

Simon Lockard came back to his house on the River Clyde. He changed his name to Locheart or Lockhart and added to the arms of his family a heart within a lock, with the motto, "*Corda serrata pando*". Up to this point the story of Douglas, the heart of Bruce, and Simon Lockard is well authenticated. But now the Lockhart family tradition takes over. I feel I cannot do better than quote once again from *The Scottish Tourist*.

The author writes of Simon Lockard:

Having taken prisoner a Saracen prince, his wife came to pay his ransom, and in counting it out, she dropped this jewel, and eagerly snatched it up; on which Lockard insisted that without the jewel being included in the ransom, he would not part with his captive; and she, finding him determined, at length yielded it up, and told him of its virtues, namely, that it cured diseases in men and cattle.

Many are the cures said to have been performed by it; and certain it is, that people came from all parts of Scotland, and even from England, to procure the water in which the stone had been dipped.

It is said that when the plague was last at Newcastle (this, as I've said, was written in 1830), the corporation sent for the *penny* and gave a bond for a large sum in trust for it; so convinced were they of its miraculous efficacy, that they offered to pay the penalty and keep the penny, which, however, was declined by the proprietor.

The most remarkable and best attested of its cures is said to have been that performed, upwards of a century ago, upon Lady Baird of Saughtonhall, near Edinburgh, who, having been bit by a mad dog, exhibited symptoms of hydrophobia. The loan of this penny was procured, and the lady daily drank and bathed in the water in which it was dipped for some weeks, until her recovery was completed— a striking example of the influence of imagination over disease! The stone was always used by dipping it in water, afterwards drank by the patient, and applied to the wound or sore.

As far as I can discover, the Lee Penny has not been used to cure anything (in public, at any rate!) for many years, and it is now regarded in Scotland in the same legendary way as the Fairy Flag of the Clan MacLeod in Dunvegan Castle on the Isle of Skye. The Fairy Flag is reputed to have the power of saving the MacLeods from disaster when it is waved. But that power runs to only three wavings and, according to Dame Flora MacLeod of MacLeod, the present chieftain of the clan, it has already been waved twice. On each occasion the clan was saved. Now, however, the Fairy Flag is kept in a frame under glass, and it does not seem likely that it will be waved a third time.

It's interesting to note that, although legend has it that the flag was given to a MacLeod chief by the fairies, experts on such matters think that it is of oriental manufacture. It may well be that, like the Lee Penny, it came from the East.

However, this is a diversion from the road leading out from Kirkfieldbank. On either side of the road are the orchards, full of apple and plum trees. Behind the orchards are the hothouses, full of tomatoes and flowers. The road is high and the Clyde runs far below it. But there is a path down to Stonebyres Hydro-Electric Station, built near once-famous falls.

The road from Kirkfieldbank to Garrion Bridge, near Hamilton is a comparatively quiet one, except at the height of the flourish and fruit seasons. There are few buses and it can be a pleasant walk out of season. There is a string of little villages above and beside the Clyde, and each of them has its champions from Glasgow and the Lanarkshire industrial belt, who will aver that the clachan of their choice is the finest jewel in the Clydeside necklace.

Some swear by Hazelbank, and I'd put it high on the list myself if only it had a pleasant inn or a good hotel. But Hazelbank is 'dry', as we say in Scotland, because we don't count tea as wet. From Hazelbank a road runs up to Blackford on the main road between north and south, and on to Strathaven (pronounced 'Strayven') on the River Avon, one of the many Clyde tributaries hereabouts. Strathaven is a typical little Lanarkshire town, with some narrow streets, the ruins of a fifteenth-century castle, and brand-new buildings sticking up in the middle of the old ones. To some people it is a place of pilgrimage because Sir Harry Lauder built Lauder Ha' there and spent his retirement in Strathaven. Now the charm of the burgh is threatened by road developments.

The road from Hazelbank runs downhill to the next village, Crossford, whose name indicates its origin. Instead of a ford, however, there is a bridge in the middle of the village, and across the Clyde you can get to Braidwood and Carluke on the main road north. Carluke, a solid little town with a great reputation for jam-making, is another place associated with Sir William Wallace; it was there he was appointed Guardian of Scotland.

In Crossford you see the Tillietudlem Hotel, owned by a

renowned Scottish footballer, George Young, who was captain of Scotland and Rangers for a wheen of years. Indeed, one of the sights of the hotel is a glass case containing his caps and various football trophies presented to him. But the reason I direct your attention to the Tillietudlem Hotel is not because of the distinguished athlete. It's because most people imagine Tillietudlem to be a real name, and they don't realize that Sir Walter Scott invented it.

On the steep banks of the Nethan Water, another Clyde tributary, stands the ruins of Craignethan Castle, once a strong tower belonging to the noble family of Hamilton.

Craignethan (the word means 'the rock of the Nethan') was built by Sir James Hamilton early in the sixteenth century. I have referred to "the noble family of Hamilton". They were noble enough to have King James V of Scotland as a guest at the wedding in Craignethan of James, Master of Somerville, eldest son of Lord Somerville, to Agnes, daughter of Sir James Hamilton.

The castle was strong enough to be a place of safety for Mary Queen of Scots after she had escaped from Lochleven Castle and sought refuge with the Hamiltons. Her escape, though, was but the beginning of her end.

Sir Walter Scott was entranced by Craignethan and, in *Old Mortality*, renamed it Tillietudlem Castle, as I have already indicated.

Not long ago I had a visit from an American whose name was Jarvie. He asked if I would help him to find out if he was related to the famous Bailie Nicol Jarvie of Glasgow. He was most disappointed when I told him that there never was a Bailie Nicol Jarvie in Glasgow. He was invented by Sir Walter Scott for *Rob Roy*.

A railway company actually built a Tillietudlem Station, not far from Craignethan Castle. This was because of public demand. The people who read *Old Mortality* believed there was a place named Tillietudlem, so the railway company obligingly gave them one, and in due course houses were built around the station and the place became officially Tillietudlem. But the interest gradually died out and Tillietudlem Station was abandoned a long time ago. I'm glad to say that I was one of the travellers to Tillietudlem in my day, and I still recollect being the only passenger to get off the train at Tillietudlem.

Craignethan Castle itself looks mysterious as it hangs on a crag over the dark burn below. Perhaps that is why there are stories about the phantom armies which some people have seen battling in Nethan glen. In various parts of Scotland there are similar stories about ghostly warriors engaged in mortal combat, and the odd thing is that the places where they have been seen (or thought to have been seen) have seldom been the sites of actual battles long ago.

From Crossford to Rosebank there are no more hills and the road is not far from the river. Various small paths run down to the Clyde, and fishermen get to it through fields and by hothouses and past cattle. This part of the Clyde was the original orchard country. It is very sheltered and you have only to see the marvellous display of roses at Rosebank to realize how suitable the soil is for flowers and fruit. Indeed, Rosebank is one place in Scotland which lives up to its name.

Before you reach Rosebank you pass the elaborate entrance to what was once the estate of Milton Lockhart. Above the red sandstone archway leading to a bridge across the Clyde is a rope carved in stone. It twists as it might twist in hemp and is much admired locally as a distinctive piece of sculpture. Indeed, Clydesdale people will take you specially to see it, and it is your duty to admire it.

From the rope it's not long to the roses. Rosebank vies with Hazelbank as the most popular place for tourists in the orchard country. I have my own choice, as you will see soon. But Rosebank is a comparatively modern village, although it doesn't look it. Visitors are entranced by the sight of a police station embowered in roses and by the Popinjay Inn.

When I knew the Popinjay first, it was famous for its roses too. But such are the advances of civilization that the beautiful rose garden on one side has been turned into a car park. The inn has a high reputation, and if you want to eat or sleep there you are as well to book in advance. Although it is in the heart of the country, it is not far from great industrial centres, and where there are great

industrial centres there are industrialists who want bed and breakfast, lunch and dinner.

The Popinjay Inn is yet another place in the orchard country
which owes its name to Sir Walter Scott. According to Scott, a
popinjay was a peculiar kind of target for Scottish archers. It
consisted of an effigy of a parrot (or a bird resembling a parrot)
on the top of a tall pole. Instead of aiming their arrows horizont-
ally at a ground target, the archers had to aim almost vertically.
Every now and then a group of archers will descend on the
Popinjay Inn, erect a popinjay and have a competition among
themselves.

From Rosebank you go to the hidden village of Dalserf, by far
the oldest of all the villages between Lanark and Hamilton along
this road. On the way you pass the entrance to Mauldslie Castle.
This estate was Crown land in the time of John Baliol, King of
Scots, who pledged it to Philip the Fair of France. However,
nobody paid any attention to the pledges of John Baliol, and there
was never a French claimant for the land. Robert the Bruce took
over the district when he assumed the crown of Scotland and,
being a most religious man, granted ten merks sterling out of his
mills at Mauldslie to keep a lamp constantly burning upon St.
Machute's tomb at Lesmahagow.

Perhaps I should explain that Lesmahagow is a strange little
town, not so very far from Lanark but on the other side of the
Clyde. I have quoted 'St. Machute' on one authority, but another
suggests that the saint's name was St. Mahago, a sixth-century
Christian missionary.

Of Mauldslie Castle let me quote an account of the early
nineteenth century.

It was built in 1793 from a design of Robert Adam. It extends 104
feet in length, by fifty-eight over the walls, and is flanked by
towers, the whole finely proportioned and beautifully ornamented.
The roof is of admirable workmanship. Seated on a headland, pro-
jecting from the north bank far into the river, it commands on each
side an extensive view of the valley, and presents a most magnificent
appearance, especially when viewed from the west.

It was the seat of the last Earl of Hyndford. There is no
Mauldslie Castle now. I mention this because, in our next
chapter, we come to a part of the River Clyde where there
were once many great houses. But the glory (if you can call it
that) has departed.

If you are passing the entrance to Mauldslie Castle in a car, you
may well pass the entrance to the village of Dalserf without
knowing it. There is, to be sure, a small signpost, but—unless it
has been changed since last I saw it—you could easily miss it.

But take the side road to the right and you will find yourself in a
small, enchanting place, with little cottages clustering along the
way and flowers everywhere. The road leads down to what was
once an important ford across the Clyde. It passes the sixteenth-
century kirk, which is small and simple and well worth seeing.
Don't be misled by the date on the clock tower, which would
make you think the place was nineteenth century.

Dalserf was once by far the most important village in the whole
of this district. One of its natives told me, "There was a time when
Dalserf had a population of 2,000 and seven pubs. Now we've a
population of fifty and no pub!"

We come out of the orchard country of the Clyde along a dark
avenue of trees. Below, on the right, are the fishermen in the river.
We arrive at a crossroads and there is the Garrion Bridge. Until
recently there were also the Garrion Mills on the far side, pro-
claiming their slogan—"For man, beast, fowl, better canna be."
Unfortunately this boastful slogan is no longer true. Though there
were meal mills there for over 800 years, the buildings have now
been demolished.

Garrion Bridge is an important junction on the Clyde. We have
come up on the road from Lanark. On the right is the road to
Wishaw and Motherwell. Straight ahead is the way to Hamilton.
And on the left is the road to Larkhall and the motorway.

Perhaps the greatest tribute to Garrion Bridge is what it says
about itself. On one side of the bridge there is a tablet which runs,

In testimony of Respect and Gratitude to General Sir James Stewart
of Coltness and Westshield, Bart., In whose Patriotic zeal for the
improvement of his Country the Bridge Originated. And by whose

liberal Contributions United with those of Mrs. Katherine Birnie Mitchelson of Broomhill and The Revd. John Scott, D.D. Minister of Avendale, It was happily completed in the year 1817 At a time when there was no safe passage across the Clyde from Lanark to Bothwell. The other Contributers [*sic*] erected this tablet. Erected by Ken Mathieson of Glasgow.

No doubt that 1817 bridge was the beginning of the end of the importance of Dalserf. Who would bother crossing the ford when there was a fine new bridge?

We don't cross Garrion Bridge. We go straight ahead into the Black Country of the Clyde.

CHAPTER VI

THE BLACK COUNTRY

The 'Black Country' of the Clyde is not as black as it is painted. True, when you come up the Hamilton road from Garrion Bridge, you look across the river and there, on a long, high bluff, are the skyscrapers, the chimneys, the cooling towers and the factories of Motherwell and Wishaw. But below them in the valley of the Clyde there are still trees and farms and hothouses and estates. And even in the middle of the industrial complex there are signs of the old days when the two towns were four separate little villages in the heart of the country.

Indeed, the sight of Motherwell and Wishaw spread out on that bluff may not be beautiful, but it is spectacular. Nearer at hand across the Clyde are two stately homes. The one in the open is Cambusnethan Priory, once the home of Sir John Craig, managing director for so many years of the firm which, so to speak, turned this countryside 'black'—Colvilles, the steelmakers. The Priory is now the setting for elaborate mediaeval banquets with mead, minstrels and buxom serving wenches.

The other you can see only in the winter time when the surrounding trees are bare. It is Dalzell House, once a noble residence, latterly a private school, and now awaiting a decision by Motherwell and Wishaw Town Council as to its future. By the way, you will sometimes see Dalzell spelt Dalziel (or even Dalyell, if you count the M.P. of that name). Just to make it harder the accepted Scots pronunciation, however the name is spelt, is 'Dee-ell'! 'Dal zell' is archaic Scots for 'I dare'.

Our quiet road goes up to join the busy motorway, the main way south from Glasgow. This motorway has changed the whole appearance of this part of the country. When I last walked up the Clyde I had to leave the river at the bridge which connects Hamilton with Motherwell and walk through Hamilton and along what was then the main road towards the little side road to Lanark. I could see the Clyde winding in the distance and made one or two forays down to its banks to find out if I could follow them. But these forays were unsuccessful and I gave them up and kept to the road, which meant I saw the river only in the distance until I got near Garrion Bridge.

But now the motorway runs for a considerable distance right beside the Clyde. And that means that the walker's chance of keeping near the river is non-existent because, as you know, pedestrians are barred from motorways. So if you have a car you can follow the Clyde for quite a way here. If you walk, you walk into Hamilton by the main road that I took, and you can hardly even see the river now for the motorway in between.

On the left is the high wall surrounding the High Parks of Cadzow, once part of the great estates of the Dukes of Hamilton. At one time this was part of the vast Caledonian forest, and there are still remnants of it to be seen. It was said of the trees in Cadzow Forest that they took 1,000 years to grow, 1,000 years to flourish and 1,000 years to decay. In that case, some of them are undoubtedly on their last 1,000 years.

I was taken on a tour of the High Parks by a noted Hamilton historian, A. G. Miller. He was retired and considerably older than I was, but he stepped it out in a way that I had difficulty in following. We went up by the golf course and some farmland to the four sandstone towers of Chatelherault. This French château was built by one of the Dukes of Hamilton in 1732 in imitation of the château of the same name at Poiteau. It was a 'folly', of course, though it was used as a shooting lodge.

The Hamilton family are connected directly or through marriage with most of the royal and noble families of the Continent. The Dukedom of Chatelherault was conferred by King Henry II of France on the second Earl of Arran, who had obligingly arranged the marriage of Mary Queen of Scots and the Dauphin of France against the wishes of King Henry VIII of

England. The Hamiltons were connected with the Arrans and had a claim on Chatelherault. Indeed, at one time the title was Duke of Hamilton and Chatelherault.

Nowadays there is a big sand quarry near the château, and the building itself is just a picturesque red ruin. It appears that the Duke of Hamilton builded his house on sand. This is all the more ironic since, as we shall soon see, another Duke of Hamilton built *his* house on coal and it perished too.

Mr. Miller took me round the gardens of Chatelherault and down a road to the River Avon, a tributary of the Clyde, which when it joins the parent river is wide enough to make people pause at the confluence and wonder which is the Clyde and which is the Avon. If you are in any doubt when you reach these parts, the answer is quite simple. The motorway runs beside the Clyde but it crosses over the Avon.

In the High Parks, however, the Avon is narrow and furious. We walked down the road to a bridge high over the rushing river. I had a strange foreboding that, once again, my nerve was going to be tested. And I was right. Mr. Miller led me across the bridge to the ruins of Cadzow Castle. So many castles of the Clyde stand on top of a chasm. Doubtless this was for defensive purposes, and the situation makes things difficult even today. Cora Castle on the Falls of Clyde is built on a precipice. Craignethan Castle overhangs the Nethan Burn. Now I found that Mr. Miller, hopping around the ruins like a mountain goat, was leading me into dangerous paths.

The day was wintry and wet, and these paths were muddy and slippery. I didn't mind that so much as the fact that the paths often hung over a sheer drop to the boiling river below. And all the time Mr. Miller was giving me a non-stop history of Cadzow Castle.

In Hamilton there is a place called Eddlewood and in the thirteenth century it was owned by Sir Gilbert de Bellemont, a grandson of the third Earl of Leicester. When he was in Scotland he preferred to be known as Sir Gilbert of Eddlewood. He was a friend of Robert the Bruce when that knight was doing homage at the court of Edward I of England, 'the Hammer of the Scots',

The orchard country, with the village of Crossford below

Robert Burns walked over this bridge to visit the kirk at Lamington

who insisted that Scotland belonged to him and so put Sir William Wallace to torture and death in London as a traitor.

Bruce was playing a double game, as a courtier of King Edward's and as a claimant for the crown of Scotland. When things in London got too hot for him, Bruce left the court and rode north. He knew he would soon be a wanted man, so, according to legend, he got a blacksmith to reverse the shoes on his horse so that, if anyone saw his tracks, he would think Bruce was coming instead of going!

Sir Gilbert of Eddlewood was at King Edward's court when the absent Bruce fell into disfavour. One day Edward was denouncing Bruce as a traitor when Sir Gilbert made a spirited defence of his friend. This was too much for one, John de Spencer, who struck Sir Gilbert in the face. There was only one answer to this—a duel. Sir Gilbert killed John de Spencer and, like Bruce, had to flee to Scotland.

He and his servant were pursued by de Spencer's men, and, when they realized they must have rest and new horses, they stopped in a forest and persuaded two woodcutters they met to change clothes. The woodcutters in their new finery disappeared into the forest, and Sir Gilbert and his servant were sawing through an oak tree when de Spencer's men rode up. Sir Gilbert saw that his servant was nervous, so he called out in a commanding voice, "Through!", and as they finished sawing through the oak de Spencer's men rode on. Sir Gilbert was so impressed by this escape that he adopted "Through!" as his motto and put the oak and the saw into his crest.

When he was back in Scotland, Sir Gilbert joined Bruce's army of independence, and, at the Battle of Bannockburn in 1314, he was one of the seven knights who formed a personal bodyguard for the King of Scots. He was also one of the chief mourners when Robert the Bruce was buried in Dunfermline Abbey.

Naturally, Sir Gilbert of Eddlewood benefited from his close association with the King. He received land and offices and money, and he changed his name to Sir Gilbert de Hamilton. It was his son Walter who acquired the lands of Cadzow. He married Princess Mary, the eldest daughter of King James II of Scotland.

5

The road beside the Clyde through the orchard country to Lanark

Cadzow Castle was already built when Walter de Hamilton took over the lands of Cadzow. Its early origins are wrapt in mystery, but A. G. Williamson in his book *Twixt Forth and Clyde* says: "Its architecture and domestic history would seem to point to it having been built by King David the First, in 1140, as a successor to the old hunting-seat of the kings of Strathclyde on the banks of the Barncluith Burn."

It was King David I who planted many of the oaks which you can see today. The Scottish royal family lived in Cadzow Castle for many years. Among them were King Malcolm IV (known as 'Malcolm the Maiden' to his disrespectful subjects), King William the Lion, King Alexander II and King Alexander III. For a while it belonged to the 'Toom Tabard', John Baliol, who paid homage to Edward I of England. Then came the great days of Robert the Bruce and, after Bannockburn, the King of Scots gave Cadzow to Sir Walter Fitz-Gilbert or de Hamilton, the son of Gilbert of Eddlewood.

In 1445 the then Lord Hamilton changed the name from Cadzow Castle to Hamilton Castle. It was from this castle that he gave his orders for the establishment of a new town of Hamilton in 1456. Hamilton, the historian of Wishaw, wrote:

In the tyme of King James the Second, James Lord Hamilton erected here ane burgh of baronie in the midst of ane large and pleasant valley, extending from the mouth of Aven to Bothwell bridge, near 2 miles along the river [Clyde], with a pleasant burn, running through the town and gardens, now belonging to the Duke; giving out severall lands to the inhabitants to be holden of the family, reserving to themselves, the superioritie, jurisdiction, and nameing of the magistrates.

The Hamiltons became one of the most powerful noble families of Scotland. They supported Mary Queen of Scots when other Scottish nobles were against her. So it came to be that the last member of the royal family of Scotland to stay at Cadzow Castle was Mary, who was there in 1568 after escaping from imprisonment in Lochleven Castle. She went straight to the Hamiltons, who took her first to Craignethan Castle, as I have recorded, and then to Cadzow, before they decided—with the Queen, of course—to march to Glasgow to do battle with the Regent Moray's forces.

They joined· battle at what is now Langside, a suburb of Glasgow, and Mary, and the Hamiltons, lost. Thereafter, the Hamiltons were at bay for years. Cadzow Castle was often besieged, and the final attack took place in 1579. The Duke of Hamilton had left the defence of Cadzow to a cadet of his house, Captain Arthur Hamilton of Merryton. His resistance was short, the castle was captured, and Hamilton was executed in public. The Regent Morton ordered that Cadzow Castle should be pulled down.

Some twelve years later the Hamiltons were back in power, and the Duke built his great Palace on the North Haugh beside the Clyde. Cadzow Castle has lain a ruin for 400 years. But you can still see something of Cadzow, whereas there is not a stone left of Hamilton Palace.

From the ruined Cadzow Castle Mr. Miller took me to see the famous white cattle of Cadzow Forest. This is the only herd of white cattle in Scotland, and I understand there is only one other herd in the whole of Britain. They are wild cattle and said to be dangerous if provoked. Mr. Miller said he knew of a case where one of the white bulls chased a man up an oak tree and he had to stay there all night until the herd moved on in the dawn.

They looked docile enough to me. Rather smaller than most cattle and with the same sturdy aspect of Highland cattle. They were white (or off-white might be a more exact description) with dark ears, muzzles and hooves. From a distance I couldn't tell whether it was black or brown, but I'd favour black myself.

The wild white cattle have been in danger of extermination several times, and it's good to see a herd of such ancient lineage moving through such an ancient forest. Hector Boece wrote of the Caledonian Forest and its white cattle in the fifteenth century:

In this wod wes sum time quhit bullis, with crisp and curland mane, like feirs loonis, and thoucht thay seemit meek and tame in the remanent figure of that body is thay wer wild than ony uther beiztis, and had sich hatrent aganis the societe and cumpany of min, that they come nevir in the wodis nor lesuris quhair thay fand ony feit or haind thairof, and moy dayis efter, thay eit nocht of the herbis that wer twichit or handillet by men. Their bullis wer sa wild that thay were nevin tane but slight and crafty laubor, and sa impacient that, eftir thair taking, they deit for importable doloure. Als sone as ony man invadit thir bullis, thay ruschit with so terrible preis on him, that they dang him to the eord, takand na feir of houndis, scharp lancis, nor uthir maist penitrive wapintris. And thoocht thir bullis wer bred in sindry boundis of the Caledon wod, now, be continewal hunting and lust of insolent men, thay are destroyit in all party of Scotland and nane of thaim left bot allanerlie in Cumarnald.

It seems that Hector Boece would certainly be in that society today which seeks for the preservation of wild life. But about a hundred years later men were still pleading for the wild white cattle. The last herd that Boece mentions, the one at Cumbernauld, was almost exterminated when a protest was made to the King against the killing of

the quhit ky and bullis of the said forest, to the gryt destructione of the commonweil. For that kind of ky and bullis hes bein keipit thir money zeiris in the said forest; and the like was not mantenit in ony uther partis of the Ile of Albion.

We left the Cadzow cattle as the winter dark descended on the wood. Mr. Miller pointed out one or two of his favourite oaks and beeches, and took me down a path to see a tree that he regarded as unique. It was an ancient oak and the branches spread out from its top leaving a sort of hollow. In that hollow was growing a fine ash tree.

We went back down by the Avon to the sixteenth-century Dutch gardens of Barncluith, 250 feet above the river. They are a series of flowered terraces which come down from Barncluith House by the bridge which carries the road over to Hamilton. When you cross this bridge and see that beauty, you can hardly imagine that the river below goes down to join the Clyde at a place surrounded by every artifice of modern ingenuity. However, you have only to walk a little way and you are at the unprepossessing clachan of Ferniegair and you can imagine anything. You go into the town by villas, remnants of coal mines, shops, gardens, hotels and more shops to Hamilton Cross.

To reach the River Clyde once again you turn right, past the Hotel Splendid. (It was originally to be called the Splendide, but somebody told the owner that nobody in Hamilton would understand the final 'e', so it was shortened to Splendid!) This is where the interchange of the new motorway looks baffling to the eye. If you are walking through it's quite simple, and every now and then your path becomes a flyover and you get fine views of the surrounding district.

And so you reach Clyde Bridge, with the river running wide below it and the coats of arms of the two burghs facing each other on either side. The Hamilton coat of arms is a modest signboard. But at the other end of the bridge there is a triumphal arch with the coat of arms of Motherwell and Wishaw hanging from it. The supporters of this coat of arms are a steelworker and a miner and the motto is the simple one, "*Industria*".

The official guide to Motherwell and Wishaw describes it as "The centre of the Scottish steel industry—the industrial heart of Scotland—and yet a gateway to the rich orchard country of the beautiful and fertile Clyde valley". True, when William Cobbett crossed this part of the Clyde valley in 1832, he wrote:

The glen, the walks winding about on each side of it—the orchards and the fruit trees mixed among the forest trees—all these put together made me think this the place of all places in Scotland that I should like to live at.

Now, at Clyde Bridge, there is still the small public park to the right, with its warning notices about bathing and fishing. But to the left the scene has changed dramatically, for this is now Strathclyde Regional Park—of which more anon. First, we climb the hill from Clyde Bridge into Motherwell.

Motherwell today is, as befits the centre of the Scottish steel industry, bold and brash. Most people don't refer, as I have been careful in doing, to Motherwell and Wishaw. They just say Motherwell. This is not to say that Wishaw is forgotten. Indeed, Wishaw people make it quite clear that they are not Motherwell people. But, combined, there is a population of 80,000 and a great desire to make the burgh bigger and better than ever it was. It has even been suggested that Motherwell and Wishaw should combine with the ancient town of Hamilton, and then there would indeed be a new city in Scotland. But the Hamilton folk are not for it.

It's true that an old charter of King David II of Scotland refers to "the Barony of Dalyel and Modervale", and about the same time there is a reference to "Modyrwaile". The name derives from a well or pool dedicated to the Virgin Mary. Wishaw also is a very old name, starting with Waygateshaw, through Wicket-shaw and Wishawtown, to Wishaw. The original name means 'the gate in the wood'. But these were merely place names when Hamilton was a thriving town.

About the beginning of the nineteenth century there were two small villages called Motherwell and Windmillhill, and they eventually joined together. At the same time there were two small villages called Wishawtown and Allanton, and they also joined together. At that time the combined Wishaw had a bigger population than the combined Motherwell.

The country folk who lived in these villages regarded Hamilton as their centre for everything. They didn't know what was going to happen to them. A bright man called David Colville moved into the district in 1870. In the following year he had built an iron works at Windmillhill for the manufacture of malleable iron bars, angles, beams, and so on. He got the coal to run his iron works from Wishaw, where there were rich seams. Eight years later he went into steel, and workmen and their wives and families rushed to Motherwell for jobs.

As a guide to Motherwell and Wishaw says proudly,

Motherwell steel, fired by Wishaw coal, played a part in engineering adventures the world over. It will be found in bridges in remote parts of the Commonwealth, in pitheads in Africa, in railway stations at home and abroad, in public and office buildings, theatres and factories all over Great Britain and in boilers, storage tanks, pipelines and coal-cutting machines throughout the world. It shaped the hulls of the great sister ships *Queen Mary* and *Queen*

Elizabeth and has been used to create some of the vast nuclear power stations. It now sustains the fast-developing Scottish motor industry.

It has to be admitted, of course, that the Wishaw coal seams were eventually worked out, although old miners in the area have assured me that there is still plenty of coal under the ground. Wishaw had its bad times, and its amalgamation with Motherwell helped it to make the transition from coal to engineering and light industries. Colvilles today operate six big steel works at Motherwell and Wishaw. Not long ago they completed a new continuous steel strip mill at Ravenscraig at a cost of £70 million.

Although Motherwell is so thirled to steel—even the famous local football club, Motherwell F.C., are known as 'the steelmen'—there are many other industries in the burgh. Motherwell workers are assembling computers, making heavy earth-moving machinery, sports equipment, electronic controls and a host of other products needed by the modern world.

Down at Clyde Bridge there are warnings against swimming in the river. They must be for visitors, because the local people go to the local swimming baths. The new Wishaw Baths have a David Crabb Training Pool, in memory of the man who put Motherwell and Wishaw swimmers on the world map. In the past thirty years boys and girls from this burgh have represented Britain at the Olympic Games on fifteen occasions. They have held three world records, forty-seven British and 172 Scottish records, and thirty-two British and 151 Scottish championships. And I wonder if one of them ever swam in the River Clyde!

As I think I have indicated, Motherwell (in the old Scots phrase) has a good conceit of itself. And if you are apt to harp too much on its industrial and sporting sides, it's not long before someone will remind you, gently, that the conductor of the Scottish National Orchestra and one of the founders of Scottish Opera is a Motherwell man, Alexander Gibson.

I have said all this, to a certain extent, in self defence. Well, not so much in self defence as in defence of Motherwell and Wishaw. For, if you cross Clyde Bridge and make your way up the hill to Motherwell Cross, you may not be carried away with admiration for the place. It is in the process of being modernized, and in its centre there is still an uneasy mixture of the new and the late Victorian and that indeterminate period of architecture that occurred around the Twenties. (Wishaw was joined to Motherwell in 1930.)

Yet Motherwell and Wishaw have their historical places too. Camp Street in Motherwell records the fact that a Roman Camp was established there, and Watling Street ran by it down to the River Clyde at Bothwellhaugh in the valley between Motherwell and Bothwell. And if you go to Ladywell Street you can see the cope stone of the well which gave Motherwell its name. Then there is the ancient kirk of Dalziel, given to the monks of Paisley Abbey by Bishop Jocelin, the Glasgow Bishop, who also founded that famous institution, the Glasgow Fair, held (as we'll come to later) on the banks of the Clyde.

In Wishaw you may like to see Cambusnethan Old Parish Church because the Steuarts of Coltness are buried there, and particularly Sir James Steuart, a staunch Presbyterian until he met Prince Charles Edward Stuart, otherwise Bonnie Prince Charlie. He was completely captivated by the Prince, and when the 1745 Rising took place, he decided to join the Jacobites in spite of his religion. But he took a typically Scottish way of doing this.

According to Dr. Chambers in his *History of the Rebellion*, he was disposed to join the enterprise of the prince, but wished that, in doing so, he should not appear quite a free agent. His sister's husband, the Earl of Buchan, a good man, of moderate understanding, was brought by him to the same views, and they agreed with Lady Steuart's brother, Lord Elcho, that they should be seized in a public place and carried to Holyrood House, as if against their will.

Walking next day at the Cross of Edinburgh, Sir James and the Earl were seized accordingly, and conducted to the Palace. There a message was sent from an anteroom to the Chevalier, mentioning their presence. The Prince, who in the meanwhile had heard of the manner of their visit, returned for answer, that if the Earl of Buchan and Sir James Steuart came as willing partisans to befriend his cause, he should be proud and happy to see them, but not otherwise. This bluntness, though honourable to the Prince's candour, displeased Buchan, whose resolution, perhaps, had already begun to give way. He therefore made a low bow to the officer, and said—"Please inform His Royal Highness that I have the honour to be his most obedient humble servant"; after which he instantly left the Palace.

Sir James, too much offended with the Government to retrace his steps, remained to see the Prince upon the terms prescribed.

But Bonnie Prince Charlie, having led his Highland Army as far as Derby, was ill-advised by his generals, and, instead of pressing for London, where the King and Government had already made plans to flee, he turned back for Scotland. He·sent Sir James Steuart to France to ask aid from King Louis XV, and Sir James was still there when Prince Charles was defeated at the Battle of Culloden and the rising was at an end. Sir James made a turn-about once again, was pardoned and returned to his house at Coltness above the Clyde in 1763. There he settled down to write a book that was famous in its time, *Inquiry into the Principles of Political Economy*.

Now we have been through Motherwell to the end of Wishaw. If we retrace our steps to Motherwell Cross, we can return, somewhat circuitously, to the River Clyde. When we came up from Hamilton to the Cross we turned right and went to Wishaw. Now at the Cross we turn left and go past Motherwell Station and various factories to a Council housing scheme. And if we go through that scheme to a road leading down by the South Calder Water to the Clyde, we are actually following the path the Romans took when they were attempting to conquer Caledonia, stern and wild.

This road leads to a Roman bridge, built in the time of the Emperor Septimus Severus and possibly to his instructions, for he repaired and partly built Hadrian's Wall and helped to lay out Watling Street. The bridge is off the present road. It has a single arch with a span of twenty feet. It's high and narrow and has no parapets. Nervous people wouldn't like walking across it. But the Roman Armies crossed and recrossed it.

As A. G. Williamson says,

Severus crossed it; and so did his son, Caracalla; and Constantius, whose Empress, Helena, discovered the Holy Sepulchre and the wood of the true Cross; and their grandson, Constans, the son of Constantine the Great; and Theodosius; and, after Theodosius, King Arthur and every ruler of Strathclyde and Scotland during the next fifteen hundred years. It was over this bridge that the Roman legions marched when they were recalled to Rome to defend it against Alaric and his Goths.

Perhaps for the benefit of incredulous Sassenachs who have always thought that King Arthur and his Knights lived somewhere in the south of England, I should explain that there are theories in Scotland that he was one of the kings of Strathclyde, the region round the river, and that most of his doughty deeds were accomplished up and down the banks of the Clyde. I must be honest, however, and say also that in Edinburgh there is a theory that he lived in that district, and that explains why the extinct volcano in the middle of the city is known as Arthur's Seat. There are Edinburghers who will tell you that King Arthur and his court are still there, underneath the miniature mountain.

From the Roman road down into the valley you see, spread before you, the new Strathclyde Regional Park with the motorway running across it and the Clyde running through it, the strange Hamilton Mausoleum, the racecourse, Hamilton itself and the beginnings of Bothwell. Even the course of the Clyde has been altered in the making of the Park, the biggest single land reclamation ever projected in Scotland. It is costing nearly £4,500,000. The former Secretary of State for Scotland, Mr. Gordon Campbell, used a bulldozer himself to breach the river banks so that it could follow a new course alongside the M74 roadway which bisects the Park. By 1975 the first phase should be completed and the park will be an extensive complex of sports grounds and pavilions, camping and caravanning sites, and will contain Scotland's first Olympic-standard rowing lake, part of a 200-acre loch for water sports. A second phase will follow and will include an indoor sports centre.

Once you would have seen the well-populated mining village of Bothwellhaugh across the Roman bridge, but the clachan has disappeared completely in the making of the Strathclyde Park. I remember Bothwellhaugh well. I took a quite irrational liking to it—it was so uncomprisingly functional amid so much beauty. Now the whole atmosphere of that part of the Clyde has changed.

The miners of Bothwellhaugh, like all miners in this part of Scotland, were radical, humorously cynical and highly knowledgeable about their part of Clydeside. It was a Bothwellhaugh miner who reminded me that, at one time, they looked across the Clyde at the great Hamilton Palace. Much of the Duke of Hamilton's wealth came from the coal mines of the district. But it was these mines that ended Hamilton Palace. The workings spread out under the palace, and eventually it was in danger of falling to bits. So the source of the noble family's wealth was also the reason for their losing their home.

Before the coal mines were developed, Bothwellhaugh was a country estate contiguous with other estates, all owned by representatives of the large Hamilton family. Bothwellhaugh House was owned by James Hamilton, who shot the Regent Moray at Linlithgow in 1570. On one side was Boggs House, owned by the Dalzell Hamiltons, and on the other the estate of a second James Hamilton—the one who took Mary Queen of Scots from Lochleven Castle to Craignethan and then to Cadzow.

After the Battle of Langside, when the Hamiltons formed the main part of the defeated Queen's forces, six members of the family were sentenced to death. John Knox, the great Scottish Reformer, appealed on their behalf and they were pardoned. But each lost his property, including James Hamilton of Bothwellhaugh. The Regent Moray, who commanded the winning army at the Battle of Langside, was vindictive against this particular Hamilton, and he not only dispossessed him of his estate at Bothwellhaugh but also took the estate which his wife had brought him as a marriage dowry. This was Woodhouselee, near Roslin, on the other side of Scotland. Moray gave Woodhouselee to one of his favourites, Sir James Bellenden.

James Hamilton's wife was still living there when Bellenden, a big bully of a man, rode into Woodhouselee to take possession. In fact, she was in bed when he arrived; he turned her out of the house in her nightgown, and she went raving mad and died.

Sir Walter Scott was referring to her in his first ballad of Cadzow Castle when he wrote:

> What sheeted phantom wanders wild,
>   Where mountain Esk, through woodland flows,
> Her arms enfold a shadow child—
>   Oh! is it she, the pallid rose?

James Hamilton blamed the death of his wife not so much on Bellenden as the Regent Moray. He regarded him, rightly, as the arch enemy of the family of Hamilton. And so he laid his plans and, when he knew that Moray was to ride through Linlithgow, he posted himself at a convenient window with a gun and killed the Earl with his first shot.

For such a placid (or mainly placid) river, the Clyde has a remarkable record of bloodshed and internecine warfare. I am reminded of a television programme in which I took part at Cleveland, Ohio. I was being questioned about Scotland by a lady famous for her brow-beating methods.

Looking at me keenly, she said, "I've just been reading a book about your country in the old days, and it strikes me that your Scottish nobles were nothing but a set of gangsters. Is that right?"

All I could do was agree, and add that they were quite nice chaps nowadays. She looked as if she didn't believe me!

And now we must return to Clyde Bridge to see the Clyde from the Hamilton side.

CHAPTER VII

DEPARTED GLORY

Once again we stand on Clyde Bridge, between Hamilton and Motherwell, but this time, instead of looking up at Motherwell, we look across at Strathclyde Park, once the Haugh of Hamilton. A haugh is most easily translated as a meadow, or flat agricultural ground, and this is said, at 500 acres, to be the largest haugh in the whole of Scotland. The Clyde once ran round the haugh, circling the land where Hamilton Palace stood. Now it has been diverted to run parallel with the motorway. We have already visited the High Parks, with Chatelherault and Cadzow Castle and the ancient Caledonian Forest with its wild white cattle. Part of the new Strathclyde Park was known as the Low Parks, where Hamilton Palace once stood in doubtful majesty, within its 500 acres and 1400 more on the hill beyond.

All that remains of the old days are the Moat (or Mote) Hill and the Hamilton Mausoleum. As we say in Scotland, it's a far cry from the days when the Palace dominated the scene and the Dukes of Hamilton dominated Hamilton. I can remember, in my early youth, passing the long ornamental iron fence which stood between Hamilton Palace and the ordinary people. It ran right down the road from Hamilton to the Clyde. It wasn't that the Dukes of Hamilton wanted to keep the people out, for there was free access to the estate and even to the palace on suitable occasions, but a line has to be drawn somewhere. This ironwork was the line. If you want to see what it once looked like you must go up to the main road to Bothwell and Glasgow and there, in front of the new Lanarkshire College of Education, you will see part of the original fence.

The place called Hamilton was there, of course, before Hamilton Palace. On the Mote Hill—I prefer the spelling 'Mote' because I believe it marked a gathering place and not a moat round a castle—stood Netherton Cross in the fourteenth century. There was a little place called Netherton behind it, and up on the hill from which the burn descended to the Clyde was another little place called Hieton—in other words, they were the low town and the high town. But there was a mill standing on this burn, and it was known, naturally, as the Haugh Mill and the other name for Netherton was the Haugh Mill Town, pronounced locally as 'Ha' Mill Town'. When Sir Gilbert of Eddlewood was looking for a grander name, it's believed that, since he had been given all the land down to the Clyde by Robert the Bruce, he chose as his title this name, which he made Hamilton.

When you walk from Clyde Bridge into Hamilton you reach Castle Street, which takes you to Hamilton Cross. If you turn right along Cadzow Street you go over a bridge on which is a plaque saying that here "at Hieton" there was a battle between the Covenanters and the Government troops in 1667. Down below you is a public park which was once Netherton. You pass the Hamilton Public Library and the Hamilton Town Hall, liberally decorated with officially-laid stones, and come to Muir Street, leading downhill to the right. If you go down Muir Street to Castle Street and back up to the Cross, you have encompassed the original town of Hamilton, otherwise Netherton. There is nothing to be seen of Netherton, although there are still some old buildings among the new housing and the Victorian remains.

The most interesting building in Hamilton, apart, of course, from the Mausoleum, is the Burgh Museum in Muir Street. It was an inn built by a Duke of Hamilton to take the overflow from the Palace. Important guests were put up in the Palace, but lesser guests, or last-minute ones, were accommodated at the inn. The duke of the time built on an Assembly Hall, despite the kirk's criticisms, and around 1780 he used it for more popular functions than those he gave in Hamilton Palace itself.

That Assembly Hall is the main room of the Hamilton Museum

today. It was made in the Adam's style, and its fine roof has been
picked out in the Adam colours of blue and white. At one end is
a most happy—architecturally speaking—musicians' gallery. This
hall is devoted mainly to pictures and photographs of Hamilton
and the Clyde. Someone with a sense of the paradoxes of history
has chosen remarkable photographs of Hamilton Palace, outside
and inside, to contrast with the worst parts of the town. At one
moment you can look at a picture of unparalleled magnificence
which is described as "a *corner* of the Duchess's boudoir", and at
the next one which shows a line of down-and-outs crouching in
the gutter outside what was euphemistically known as a poor
men's "home".

Underneath the musicians' gallery, appropriately, are two big
glass cases commemorating one of Hamilton's favourite sons, Sir
Harry Lauder. Lauder was born in Portobello, on the east coast
of Scotland, but he spent his formative years in Hamilton, where
he was a miner. He married in Hamilton and started his theatrical
career as an amateur performer in Hamilton, and he never forgot
the town, even when he became the most highly-paid stage artist
in the world. As a youth he worked as a pony driver at Eddlewood
Colliery, and it's not too much to say that he fell in love with his
pony. When he became famous he gave a lot of time and money
to the cause of pit ponies.

When Harry Lauder heard that a committee had been formed
for promoting measures for greater safety in the mines, he made
an appeal for legislation to reform the conditions under which
the pit ponies worked. Somewhat to his surprise he received the
support of someone who might be called a neighbour of his
when he lived in Hamilton—Lady Belhaven of Wishaw House.
They got together and put up such a case for the proper treatment
of pit ponies that the appeal went to the Home Secretary and
new legislation was passed to look after them.

Some of this story, which is little known even in Hamilton,
should be represented in the new museum, and perhaps it will
be in time to come, for this is one of the most intelligently-
presented museums it has been my fortune to visit. As it is, the
Lauder cases show some of Sir Harry's most famous costumes

and properties, along with photographs and copies of songs of his outstanding acts.

Just off the Assembly Hall are the stables, with the original cobbled floor of the eighteenth century. This inn at Hamilton was a stopping place for the stage coaches between Carlisle and Glasgow. At each stage new horses took over, and the stage before Hamilton was Abington on the Clyde. So the Abington horses brought the coach in, and then they were relieved by the Hamilton horses which took it in to Glasgow. Among the exhibits in the stables is a four-in-hand coach, in brilliant-coloured trim, which is similar to the stage coaches of the period of the inn.

You can learn a lot about this part of the Clyde from the Burgh Museum, but I was particularly interested in the examples of Hamilton lace which are displayed. In 1670 the then Duchess of Hamilton brought to Scotland a number of French experts in lace-making. They taught the local women their craft, and Hamilton lace became locally famous. By 1823, however, it was nationally famous, and there were 2,500 women making lace in Hamilton. It seems strange that this craft was not carried on, but possibly the great steel and coal developments in the area overshadowed and eventually extinguished it.

Included in the museum building are the headquarters of what remains of the renowned Cameronians (Scottish Rifles) Regiment. The old kitchens of the inn have been given over to the Cameronians for a regimental museum.

The father of the present Duke of Hamilton, when he was Marquis of Douglas and Clydesdale, had a boxing ring built near the museum and fought with some of the best Scottish boxers. He had a look of the fighter about him, and in his day he was such a leader of men that it's not in the least surprising that Rudolph Hess, Hitler's deputy, thought he was the man to approach when he made his famous flight from Germany to Scotland in the last war with the idea of treating for peace.

We go down Muir Street from the museum, and to the left we can go round by the Lanarkshire Ice Rink and the Hamilton golf course to the mausoleum. But, before we reach Hamilton's

The gateway and bridge over the Clyde to Mauldslie Castle

pride and joy, let's look into the history of Hamilton Palace itself.

The building of Hamilton Palace was begun in 1591, enlarged in 1705, and it doesn't seem to have been a remarkable piece of architecture. Our two Clyde travellers, Gray and Dorothy Wordsworth recorded their opinions of it. Gray was particularly scornful and called it, in 1764, "a great, ill-contrived edifice". Much later Miss Wordsworth, fresh from marvelling at the Falls of Clyde, described it as "a large building without grandeur, a heavy, lumpish mass".

These adverse criticisms may have affected the Hamilton family for, in the early nineteenth century, they got the well-known Glasgow architect, David Hamilton, to design a 'new' palace. The rebuilding was started in 1822, and by 1830 it was impressing *The Scottish Tourist* no end.

In that year, the *Tourist* records, the population of Hamilton itself was 7,000. The town rejoiced in an academy founded in the fifteenth century, at the same time as a collegiate church. The church was pulled down and a new parish kirk built up the hill. The Netherton Cross was removed from the Mote Hill in 1926 and placed in front of it, as you can see today. There was also a town-house (now demolished), three hospitals and cavalry barracks. Despite all this, *The Scottish Tourist* recorded of Hamilton that "its general appearance is mean".

With joy the *Tourist* turned to the great building by the Clyde.

Hamilton Palace [he said] stands on a plain between the town and the river. It is a huge pile, having two deep wings at right angles with the mansion, and has an air of grandeur. His Grace the Duke of Hamilton, who is extremely partial to this seat of his ancestors, meditates great improvements about the place, and has already commenced them after a design by Hamilton of Glasgow, which harmonizes beautifully with the old part of the building.

(It's not known whether the *Tourist* had read the Gray and Wordsworth opinions.)

He goes on:

The present erection faces the northern vista, and is superb and
Among the plum blossom in the orchard country of the Clyde

magnificent. The portico consists of a double row of immense Corinthian columns, the shafts are smooth, but the capitals are most exquisitely wrought, and the corresponding pilasters rich and beautiful, being surmounted by a lofty pediment with the Ducal arms splendidly sculptured in the centre; the wings are ornamented with chaste Corinthian pilasters, in fine keeping with the portico; and a rich cornice, in harmony with the whole, runs along the building; the columns of the portico are allowed to be the largest ever used in architecture, and each are of one solid block of stone, produced on the Duke's own grounds at Dalpatrick, and weighed from the quarry upwards of 26 tons each.

By Dalpatrick the *Tourist* means Dalserf, for there were quarries near that little hidden village at one time. These great blocks of stone were twenty-five feet high and three feet three inches in diameter, and were brought into Hamilton from Dalserf on a specially constructed wagon drawn by thirty horses. Incidentally, the Palace had a frontage 265 feet in length and was sixty feet high.

However, let our *Tourist* have the last word.

The Palace, as a whole, has a noble and magnificent aspect. Strangers are at all times allowed to visit the park and the Palace without any formal application, and the interior will amply repay the tourist for the time bestowed upon the inspection. The gallery is of great extent, and is furnished with a noble collection of paintings. Among these, "Daniel in the Lions' Den", by Rubens; the "Marriage Feast", by Paul Veronese; a portrait (supposed to be the finest in the kingdom) of "William Viscount Fielding, first Earl of Denbigh, going out a shooting", by Vandyke; a large Cattle piece, by Giacomo Bassano; "Two Misers", by Matsys; and a Conversation piece, by Brouwer, are specially admired by connoisseurs. Mr. Gilpin, in particular, speaking of "Daniel in the Lions' Den", calls it "the glory of Hamilton".

Among the paintings which the *Tourist* does not mention were works by Poussin, Georgione, Corregio, Leonardo da Vinci, Kneller, Rembrandt, Titian, Salvator Rosa and Sir Joshua Reynolds. The gallery was described as "gilded and ornamented with marble, scagliola and stucco work".

Another room of Hamilton Palace contained the famous

Beckford Library, founded by the eccentric author of *Vathek* and comprising some 15,000 rare volumes. In 1882 the Duke of Hamilton needed some extra money, so there was a great auction sale of the Beckford Library. To his consternation the amount realised from the auction was a mere £400,000, which he regarded as "very poor". It recalls the story of how Alexander, 10th Duke of Hamilton, was telling one of the workmen on the mausoleum building that it would cost £130,000, and the man shook his head and said, "My Lord, it'll never pay!"

But there stands the mausoleum today, and Hamilton Palace's famous Corinthian portico, modelled by David Hamilton after the temple to Jupiter Stator at Rome, and the equally famous Tribune, with its lantern roof, and the Great Gallery, and the greatly praised black marble staircase have all gone. They had to go in the early Twenties, when the palace was threatened by subsidence and huge cracks appeared in its walls and foundations. The coal mines, mainly on the other side of the Clyde, were pushed through under the river, and Hamilton Palace became unsafe.

As I have recorded, it was pulled down in 1925. Not everything has completely disappeared, however. The marble staircase was sold in small pieces, and it's said that many an Italian cafe in Hamilton, Motherwell and Wishaw, and parts adjoining, can boast of a counter or other part of the premises which is a marble relic of Hamilton Palace.

And, apart from the Palace photographs, there are various relics in the form of furniture and staircase railings to be seen in the Hamilton Museum. We go now by the museum, the ice rink and the rolling, bright green golf course to the mausoleum. Above the trees is the slender tower of the Hamilton College of Education, looking like a pagoda skyscraper, and behind it is the even taller tower of the new Lanarkshire County Buildings. Once the headquarters of the county were situated in Glasgow, but now they are where they should be, in Lanarkshire.

Hamilton has various developments to be worked out in the Low Parks and, at that moment, the only permanent features were the mausoleum and the River Clyde.

You approach the mausoleum by a garden walk. To one side, among the trees, is a small lodge, which was once the caretaker's house. But the caretaker is now at the entrance to the golf course, and you must make contact with him if you want to see inside the mausoleum.

The building is impressive. It has been well described as "something like a Greek-Doric beehive". It is, in fact an imitation of the mausoleum of Hadrian in Rome—a great dome on a circular building surmounting a square box, sitting on three big steps. When I saw them, a part of the steps had fencing round it, and I found paving stones lifted upwards and other signs of the troubles underneath the ground. But the mausoleum itself is still untouched, and a chap who was cutting the grass round it assured me, in the good old Scottish way, "It'll see us out yet!" Since he was much younger than I was, I took it that the mausoleum had a long life ahead of it.

The visitor naturally assumes that he is looking at the front of the mausoleum. Actually, he is looking at the back, for it was built to face the Clyde. The entrance is at the back. It's a small door, looking tiny against the mausoleum's height of 200 feet. Up on the circular part of the building which supports the dome is a Latin inscription telling how Alexander, 10th Duke of Hamilton, caused it to be built.

When you go round to the Clyde side, you see an ornamental entrance to vaults on a lower level, with three bearded faces glowering across to Motherwell. Above them are two enormous stone lions, one asleep, the other awake. They are the work of a gifted young sculptor, Handyside Ritchie, who died at the early age of twenty-eight. The lions represent, respectively, death and life.

The great attraction of the mausoleum to most people is not so much the wonderfully elaborate interior as the famous echo. Now and again the B.B.C., particularly in Scotland, put on a recording of the echo in an appropriate radio programme. Listeners never seem to get tired of it. No one, so far, has been able to explain this echo. Scientists and musicians have worked out theories, but they all have flaws in them. One thing is certain and that is that the

Duke of Hamilton had to abandon the idea of using the mausoleum as a chapel because of the echo.

You hear it the moment you are inside the place, for the first thing the caretaker does is to close the little door. That causes a terrific boom and startles the unwary. Often the caretaker gets to the subject of the echo right away, because visitors are so intrigued by it that they can't listen to what he is, saying as the words rumble round the dome. The odd thing though, is, that there are seven recesses in the chapel, and if two people carry on an ordinary conversation in any of these recesses there is no echo at all.

So what the caretaker usually does is sing a stave or two. The result has to be heard to be believed, as radio listeners will testify. This one voice echoes like a choir 1,000 strong, accompanied by a really mighty organ, and not one of the kind they used to have in cinemas. Some people have suggested that, since the floor includes marble brought from an old Greek temple, there is some kind of religious magic which makes the echo. That merely indicates the fanciful effect of the echo on otherwise sensible human beings.

Once you are accustomed to the echo, you can see the magnificence of the chapel. It is a great vaulted chamber, lit by a window in the roof. There are seven arched recesses, and in the recesses on either side of the entrance are the pride of the mausoleum, the bronze doors designed by Sir John Steele. Each door has three panels, depicting Biblical subjects. The floor is made of mosaic work, and it alone cost £40,000. It consists of seventy varieties of marble, and it is said that the sources of twenty-seven of these have been exhausted. Facing the entrance to the mausoleum is the black catafalque on which the coffin of the 10th Duke lay when his time came.

The mausoleum took fourteen years to build. The walls range from four and a half to fifteen feet thick. The caretaker will tell you all this, and will add, to what he hopes is the surprise of anyone familiar with building methods, that less than a ton of cement was used in the construction.

Before we leave the Haugh of Hamilton, a word about the Mote Hill. According to Mr. A. G. Miller, the antiquarian who led me such a dance round Cadzow Castle, it looks on to the part of the River Clyde which gave the city of Glasgow part of its coat of arms.

The patron saint of Glasgow is St. Kentigern—or, to give him his popular name, St. Mungo. He established an ecclesiastical centre in Glasgow, where Glasgow Cathedral now stands, in the sixth century. At that time the King of Strathclyde was Rydderch, a strong man who thought enough of St. Mungo to consider becoming a Christian. He had a beautiful consort, Queen Languoreth, and was naturally very jealous of her.

King Rydderch's capital was at Dumbarton on the Clyde, but he had hunting seats on the Mote Hill and on the banks of the Barncluith Burn near Cadzow. Hunting up the Clyde was one of his favourite pursuits.

Well, as the old tale has it (there are several versions of the old tale, but this is my own favourite), Queen Languoreth was foolish enough to dally with one of King Rydderch's knights and went so far as to present him with a ring which the King had given her. Rydderch noticed this and decided to act. He called a hunt, and he and his knights rode along the Clyde from Dumbarton to the Mote Hill. Here, on a hot summer's day, the King proclaimed they should all rest. And, when he saw his opportunity, he went to the sleeping knight, slipped the Queen's ring off his finger, and threw it in the River Clyde.

Next day at his palace in Dumbarton he asked Queen Languoreth what had happened to the ring he had given her. Why was she not wearing it? She made some excuse and went in search of her lover. But he had found the ring was missing and, deeming discretion was the better part of valour, had departed from Strathclyde. What was the Queen to do?

She was already taking instruction in the Christian faith, and St. Mungo was her tutor. So she went to him and confessed all. He forgave her and told her that she must send a trusty man, a fisherman, to that part of the Clyde where the hunting party had rested. He was to throw in a line and bring back what he caught to St. Mungo. The trusty fisherman caught a fine salmon and brought it back to Glasgow. And the saint opened the salmon's mouth and—lo and behold!—the ring was sparkling there. St.

Mungo gave the ring to Queen Languoreth, the Queen gave it to King Rydderch, who was hoist with his own petard and couldn't say a word, and everybody lived happily ever after.

If you look at the official coat of arms of the city of Glasgow you will see two supporters in the form of salmon on either side and another salmon at the foot. Look closely at the salmon at the foot. It has a ring in its mouth!

We leave the legend and the Haugh of Hamilton and, to see the Clyde close again, we go up to the main road to Bothwell. We run, as I have said, by the last portion of ornamental railing from Hamilton Palace, along the wall by Hamilton Racecourse, one of the most popular racecourses in Scotland. From it, as from the golf course below, you see the Clyde running in its new course alongside the motorway and then turning and twisting round to Bothwell.

CHAPTER VIII

THE RIVER THAT LIVINGSTONE KNEW

The Clyde comes running down from the new Strathclyde Regional Park, sweeps under Bothwell Bridge and round the back of Bothwell. Looking south-west from the bridge, you get one of the best views of the Clyde hereabouts. The banks are high and tree-covered, and just below to your left is the Bothwell 'Lido' (so named when lidos were much of a craze in Scotland), a delightful park on the water's edge.

It was here that Wallace's Sword was recovered, after it had been taken from the Wallace Monument on the Abbey Craig at Stirling by men claiming to be Scottish Nationalists. This episode took place some years before the celebrated 'liberation' of the Stone of Destiny from Westminster Abbey, and it was intended to be a gesture of defiance to the London Government. The sword, a two-handed one and about six feet in length, was a permanent show-piece in the monument, and its removal was regarded by many people as the opposite of patriotism.

No trace of it could be found, until, more than a year later, the police received an anonymous tip-off that it was lying in the Clyde near the memorial to the Battle of Bothwell Bridge. The police found the sword with a little difficulty and it hangs once more in Wallace's Monument, which, incidentally, is the largest monument erected to one man in the whole of Britain.

This is not the Bothwell Bridge which was the scene of the battle between the Covenanters and the Duke of Monmouth's troops in 1679. The old bridge stood lower by the river and had a high arch. It was demolished, together with the toll-house which stood beside it, in 1826. The Covenanters had not much chance against King Charles's men. They had been disputing among themselves and, though they fought gallantly, they fought without direction and were easily defeated. You can see an unfinished painting of the action in the Hamilton Museum.

Some 400 Covenanters were killed and about 1,500 taken prisoner. Monmouth's dragoons chased them into the uplands around the Clyde, and many of them took refuge in Cadzow Forest. It was at this point that the Duchess of Hamilton, known as the 'Good Duchess' Anne, sent a request to Monmouth "not to disturb the game in my coverts". The Duke took the hint and called off the hunt. Indeed, his magnanimity to the Covenanters didn't appeal at all to those really professional Covenanter chasers, Dalzell and Claverhouse.

On the Bothwell side of the bridge there has been considerable road widening and the Battle memorial has been moved back from its original position at the corner of the roads which lead to Bellshill on the right and Bothwell on the left. Here the Cameronian regiment held an annual conventicle in memory of the Battle of Bothwell Brig, but, since the Cameronians have been disbanded, except for one or two Territorial companies, the future of such memorial services seems doubtful.

At Bothwell the river becomes elusive once again. There is a back road which allows you occasionally to make a sortie to the Clyde, but I suggest that you will enjoy yourself more just walking through the pleasant little town of Bothwell. There is nothing particularly remarkable about it—villas, shops, inns, a school—until you are nearly out of it, when you come to Bothwell St. Bride's Parish Church.

The kirk is a handsome red sandstone building but, when you walk through the churchyard to it, you find that it is really two churches, an old and a new, joined in the centre by a square clock tower. The old part, the choir, goes back to the fourteenth century with doors and windows of Norman type. It is about seventy feet in length and thirty-nine in breadth and was built by a master-mason named Thomas Tron. Among the tombs in the choir is one showing the mason's square, and this may very well be Thomas Tron's.

The Earl of Douglas, 'Archibald the Grim', founded this church in 1398 and is buried here. There are also memorials to two of the earls of Forfar, one of whom died at Stirling from wounds he received at the Battle of Sheriffmuir. You will see the names of Oliphant and Murray among the tombs, for these were two important families in this part of Scotland.

With so much of death around, it's interesting to recollect that a great wedding took place in this church in the year 1400. In that year Prince David, Duke of Rothesay, married Lady Marjorie Douglas. Prince David was heir to the throne of Scotland and so held the title of Duke of Rothesay. (Prince Charles holds it today). The prince and princess did not live happily ever after. Prince David quarrelled with his bride's family, the powerful Douglases. They determined to get rid of him and soon worked out a plot with the prince's uncle, the Duke of Albany. The duke wanted rid of David because he was heir to the throne, and Albany had other ideas about the King's successor.

So it happened that, when Prince David was riding to St. Andrews with a few attendants, they were surrounded by a much superior force. The attendants were sent packing, and the prince was removed from his charger to a cart horse and led through a thunderstorm to Falkland. There he was thrown into a dungeon and kept there without food. At first the governor's daughter smuggled food in to the Prince by pushing pieces of oatcake through a crack in the walls. Another young woman came to his rescue and gave him milk from her own breasts by passing long straws through a crevice in the dungeon walls. Both these girls were discovered in the act of aiding the Prince and were immediately put to death.

Prince David lived for fifteen days. He died in March 1402 of starvation. It was found that, in the extremity of hunger, he had gnawed his own flesh. But the Duke of Albany had it publicly announced that he had died of dysentery, and his jackals in the Scottish Parliament confirmed this.

Sir Walter Scott used his knowledge of Bothwell St. Bride's Church in *Marmion*. He called it "the kirk of St. Bride of Bothwell". Archibald the Grim dedicated the church to St. Bride, or

St. Bridget. She was the daughter of an Ulster Prince, born about the year 452 near Dundalk. She renounced the world and lived in a cell under an oak at Kildare. Incidentally, the Douglas family had a particular affection for St. Bride. Their ancient church at Douglas is also St. Bride's.

In the churchyard near the road is a highly-coloured memorial to Joanna Baillie, a poetess much admired by Scott. She was born at Bothwell Manse in 1762. She died at Hampstead aged eighty-nine. Among the tributes paid to her on this memorial is, "Nearly seventy years of her life was spent in London, but she retained a Scottish heart to the end." A number of her verses are inscribed on the fancy monument, and they include lines written to her sister, which run:

> Then as we paddled barefoot side by side
> Among the sunny shallows of the Clyde.

To get to the sunny shallows of the Clyde once again, the best way is to go straight ahead along the main road until you see a sign on a little road leading down to the left. This is Blantyre Mill Road, and another sign will show you that this is the way to the Livingstone Memorial at Blantyre. The wall on the right is the boundary wall of the Bothwell castle estate, now a mixture of the ruined castle itself, a golf course, a new housing complex intended for people who are well-off, and pleasant parkland. But we go down the steep road to the river, noting for the first time on the banks of the Clyde that the benefits of civilization, the improvement in educational methods, and the invention of the aerosol paint sprayer have arrived.

Plastered stupidly along the wall and on any other available space is the valiant message, "Tyre Rule", alternated occasionally by "Tyre O.K." This is not an advertisement for motor tyres. It is the slogan of a Blantyre gang of juvenile delinquents, presumably the same brave morons who threw a stone through the sign in Blantyre main street showing the way to the David Livingstone Memorial. These slogans are a blight upon the scene, but, as a Glaswegian, I shouldn't talk. Aerosol work gets much worse as you go into Glasgow along the Clyde.

Originally this road was made for people in Hamilton, Bothwell and Uddingston who worked in the Blantyre Mills on the other side of the Clyde. Blantyre Mills were run by the notable David Dale of Glasgow on the same lines on which he ran his mills at New Lanark. Many of the workers came from Blantyre, but those on the right bank of the Clyde used this road, which ran down to a ferry, where a man in a boat charged a halfpenny for crossing the river. It ran from half past five in the morning until 10.30 p.m. which will give you some idea of the hours worked in the mills in those days.

The ferry was superseded by a suspension bridge in 1852, and this was known as the Maik Brig or the Bawbee Brig, because there was still a charge of a halfpenny to cross to the other side of the Clyde. 'Maik' and 'bawbee' are old Scots words denoting a halfpenny. When I crossed that "very beautiful new suspension bridge" in 1941 there was still a toll-house and a notice board which read, "Fares: all persons crossing either way pay one half-penny also cycles and prams one halfpenny." By 1941, of course, the toll-house was empty, and there was no charge for crossing the bridge.

There were still important coal mines in this district, particularly on the Blantyre side of the Clyde, and the National Coal Board demolished the Maik Brig in 1949 and put up a new bridge at the same point, which they opened in 1952, exactly one hundred years after the original Maik Brig was opened. Nowadays the bridge is free and is used to some extent by people who live on one side of the Clyde and have their work on the other. But its principal purpose is to convey people from the Bothwell side over to the Scottish National Memorial to David Livingstone, a memorial which attracts not fewer than 40,000 visitors a year.

In the old days of the Maik Brig the people who crossed the Clyde would see the spreading Blantyre Mills and the model village designed by David Dale's son-in-law, Robert Owen. Some of the mills have gone, and all that remains of the model village is the group of cream-coloured tenements which were once part of the Shuttle Row. This is where David Livingstone, missionary, explorer and consul, was born in the year 1813. You can still see the very room in which he was born, and the whole area has been turned into a remarkable memorial to the Blantyre boy who was eventually to be buried in honour at Westminster Abbey.

David Livingstone was born on 19th March 1813, on the banks of the River Clyde. He went to school in Blantyre, but at the age of ten he started work. He was employed as a 'piecer' in the cotton mills. His working day was from 6 a.m. to 8 p.m. with time off for breakfast and dinner. And then he went to night school to 'improve' himself.

His parents saw that he was unusually intelligent, so they scraped and saved to send him to Glasgow University. His sisters worked in the mill too, and they gave money from their small wages to keep David at the University. He studied medicine and theology in Glasgow and was inspired to become a missionary. Under the auspices of the London Missionary Society he went out to Africa in 1840, and for sixteen years he worked as a medical missionary among the natives of Bechuanaland.

After these sixteen years, spent mainly in the one area of Africa, his restless spirit asserted itself. He decided to carry his missionary work, his desire for exploration, and his anti-slavery campaign right across Africa. He set out from Bechuanaland in 1852 and was the first European to cross Africa from west to east. He made this journey of 4,300 miles mainly on foot. Then he made a safari back again and, taking a somewhat different route, discovered the famous falls which he named after Queen Victoria.

When David Livingstone returned to Britain in 1857 for his first furlough, he was hailed as a great explorer and fêted everywhere. He stayed in this country for only a year, and then went back to Africa for his second great safari, on the Zambesi River. His avowed purpose was to open up this part of Africa to "Christianity and Commerce". In Victorian days these two somewhat dissimilar objectives were considered quite compatible.

Livingstone started his third great African journey in 1866, when he made a trek into the interior of the continent to the Great Lakes. It was then that he disappeared from human ken and the British journalist, H. M. Stanley, set out to seek him on behalf of a New York newspaper. The famous sentence, "Dr. Livingstone, I presume?" was spoken at Ujiji in 1871—if it was ever spoken at all, because there are now professional doubters of all our favourite legends, and some of them say that this much quoted-greeting was not uttered at the time, but thought up later.

Pleas were made to David Livingstone to return to this country, but he was dedicated to his beloved Africa and refused to leave, even when he became seriously ill and was doctoring himself with inadequate medicines. In the early morning of 1st May 1873, in a small grass hut at Ilala, his African followers found Livingstone kneeling apparently in prayer beside his bed. He was dead.

Susi and Chumah, who led the Africans who were faithful to Livingstone, took out the explorer's heart and buried it under a tree at Chief Chitambo's village at Ilala. But the tree decayed, and the Africans cut it down and replaced it with an obelisk which stands at Ilala to this day.

Now Livingstone's body had to be taken home, and it must be embalmed for the long journey. Susi and Chumah embalmed the body using two or three stones of salt and a bottle of brandy from Livingstone's medicine chest. Then they wrapped it in calico, sealed it in myonga bark, and sewed it up in sailcloth to resemble a bale of merchandise. In this part of Africa a dead body was considered unlucky, so Livingstone's legs were bent inwards at the knees so that no one could recognize the bale as a corpse.

Susi led his small party, carrying the body, for more than 1,500 miles, often through hostile country, to Zanzibar. The journey took them nine months. And from Zanzibar the body of Livingstone was brought back to Britain and to Westminster Abbey.

It's odd to look at the Shuttle Row, overhanging the Clyde, and to think that the great Livingstone story started here. These thousands of people who come to Blantyre every year are from all over the world. A great many are coloured people who were converted to Christianity by the spiritual descendants of David Livingstone. And you find, when you enter the tenement, that you are in a sort of shrine, a shrine to one man's courage and his religion.

When David Livingstone was a small boy there were twenty-four families living in the 'single ends' of this building. A 'single end' was, in fact, a single room. Outside the tenement were the lavatories, the washhouse and bleaching green, the school, a general store and the manager's house. These buildings have all gone, with the exception of the school, which is now the tea-room for visitors. Shuttle Row was surrounded by a high wall with a gate, and the gate was closed every night at ten o'clock. There was a watchman on duty, and the row had its own scavengers and, very important, a Funeral and Widows Society. By paying a penny a week you could ensure that your funeral would not let the family down!

As you go to the entrance to the Livingstone Memorial, which is, in essence, just the Shuttle Row, you see between two small towers concealing spiral staircases a plaque which says, "The children of the Sunday Schools of Scotland by their gifts bought and partly restored this property which was opened on 5th October, 1929 by H. R. H. the Duchess of York."

The Duchess of York, of course, is now the Queen Mother. Blantyre people still remember that a small boy who was a descendant of David Livingstone was picked to present the key to the duchess so that she could perform the official opening ceremony. The key was placed in a presentation box, so that both key and box would be a memento of the occasion for the duchess. But, when the small boy was urged forward to make the presentation, he took the key out of the box, handed it over to the Duchess of York, and retreated with the box!

The Shuttle Row was already thirty-three years old when David Livingstone was born, but it was still regarded in advance of its time as far as housing weavers and other working people were concerned. As you go up the spiral staircase to the top floor you will see 'jaw-boxes' in the turret wall. Waste water was thrown into these jaw-boxes and this was the only sanitary arrangement in the building. Water was brought from a well near the mill gates.

The single-ends have been turned into a chain of museum pieces throughout the tenement. First there is the Ancestry Room, with pictures showing where David's father, Neil Livingstone, lived and how the family developed. Then there is the Working Man's House about 1813, with a meal barrel in which the family's stock of oatmeal (porridge was one of the main dishes of Scotland, and was not confined to breakfast time) was kept.

Then comes the Birth Room. In the bed recess on the right David was born. Most of the furniture and articles on show were there when Livingstone was a boy. The whole family of father, mother, three boys and two girls lived in this one room, ten feet by fourteen feet. A guide to the memorial says, "The fact that decency and self-respect could be retained under the circumstances gives food for much thought."

In the Youth Room the painter, A. E. Haswell Miller, exhibits eight pictures showing episodes in David Livingstone's early career. The first is "The Barred Door", and you see the youthful David curled up asleep outside the door of his family's single-end. His father was a real Old Testament character and had laid it down that all the family were to be indoors by a certain time, which was even earlier than the 10 p.m. when the Shuttle Row gate was closed. One night young David came home in plenty of time to get through the gate but not early enough for his father's rule. The door to the single-end was already locked. David didn't even bother to knock. He knew he was wrong, so he just lay down on the doorstep and did his best to sleep until morning.

Other paintings show how he studied by candlelight at midnight (this was not against his father's rule), how he read books propped up against his loom while he worked as a weaver, to the time when he said goodbye to his family on the Broomielaw, the little steamer port on the Clyde in the heart of Glasgow.

The Blantyre Room has a model showing what Low Blantyre and the Mills looked like in the nineteenth century, together with portraits of such eminent men as David Dale and Father Gallacher. David Livingstone was a Protestant, but he went to Father Gallacher, a Roman Catholic priest, to learn Latin and other subjects. There's also a picture of the celebrated 'Paraffin' Young, the man who invented a method of extracting oil from shale. He was a fellow student of Livingstone's at the Andersonian College

Angler on the weir near Garrion Mill

in Glasgow, and later, when he became a very rich man, he financed David's expeditions in Africa.

As you go through one room after another you see the story of Livingstone's life spread before you in pictures, writings, relics, maps and models. It's rather much to take in on one visit, and I found myself recollecting afterwards some rather odd specimens from the museum—the cast of Livingstone's left arm bone crushed by the lion which attacked him, a baby crocodile shot by Livingstone, the explorer's consular cap (it's explained that he "valued uniform because of the prestige it gave him with the Arabs and African Tribes"), a casket containing the Freedom of London and a slave stick cut from a boy's neck by Livingstone himself.

But the one insignificant-looking little relic that perhaps appealed to me most was described as "BOOK MARK. Part of a baker's 'poke' (paper bag) with a picture of Hamilton Palace. The missionary had apparently used this as a book mark for many years." It's strange to think of David Livingstone, in the heart of Africa, looking at a picture, a much crumpled picture no doubt, of Hamilton Palace on the banks of the River Clyde.

Outside in the wide-spreading grounds of the memorial, much used by picnic parties from organizations interested in David Livingstone, there is a model of an African hut, and the World Fountain, designed by C. D'O. Pilkington Jackson. This globe of the world is made of marble and bronze and it is so orientated that it shows the continent on which, at any time, the sun is shining.

From the top of the memorial grounds you can see across the Clyde to the ruins of Bothwell Castle among the trees on the other side. And from these grounds, along the Blantyre side of the river, you come to the even more ruinous Blantyre Priory. But it's too difficult to get along the banks and to see Blantyre Priory at close quarters, and you must go up from the Livingstone Memorial into Blantyre itself and take the road that runs down by the remains of Blantyreferme Colliery to the Red Brig across the Clyde.

I once called Blantyre "rather drab" in print and was suitably rebuked by the inhabitants of the village. They take themselves

7

The tenement above the Clyde at Blantyre, where David Livingstone was born

The Clyde runs by Greyfriars, a house owned by the Capuchin Franciscan Friars

very seriously in all the places along the Clyde, but tend to get ever more serious as the river winds round to Glasgow. It's as if they were preserving their identity against that great civic monster of a place.

I can't resist quoting a very sensible and thoughtful letter which was sent to my editor (of *The Evening Times*, Glasgow) by Mr. R. Smith of Blantyre. In a postscript he said:

> I agree with Jack House, Blantyre is drab if one sticks to the Main Street. It's almost as drab as Glasgow, though not so noisy. There are some beautiful spots in Blantyre, but what would Jack House know of these? One cannot see Blantyre in half an hour, nor any other place for that matter.

Well, of course, I don't think that Glasgow is drab, but we'll let that flee stick to the wa'.

I have seldom gone into the origins of names along the Clyde, for the good reason that there is such confusion about derivations. Let Mr. Smith's letter prove just this.

> There has [he wrote] been a certain amount of conjecture, confusion, contention and contradiction among the various scribes over the meaning of the word [Blantyre].
>
> In the *Statistical Account of Scotland* (1785) the Rev. Henry Stevenson states that the word comes from the Gaelic and means 'a warm retreat', being descriptive of the low lying and sheltered position of the original settlement on the banks of the Clyde.
>
> In the *Annals of Blantyre* the Rev. Stewart Wright disagrees and states that the name, also from the Gaelic, means 'field of the holy men', and refers to the monks of the old Blantyre Priory.
>
> In the *New Statistical Account of Scotland* (1960) the Rev. A. McKenzie decries the above and asserts that the name (also from the Gaelic!) means 'land of Blane', an Irish monk who is said to have brought Christianity to various parts of the country in the sixth century and whose passage is marked by such place names as Strathblane and Dunblane.
>
> In a contribution to the *History of Lanarkshire*, James A. Wilson suggests that the word is Blaentir, is British, Welsh or Cymric and means a promontory, being descriptive of the northern end of the parish round which the Clyde flows. He confirms this by stating that the words Cambuslang and Rutherglen (which we come to later

along the Clyde) means 'the crooked land' and 'the serrated land' respectively; in each case the words suggest the most prominent feature of each parish in relation to the winding of the Clyde.

The 'warm retreat' suggestion is highly unlikely for one or two reasons. Certainly no palm trees ever grew in Blantyre.

Despite the fact that one of our schools is named after St. Blane, there is no evidence, except wishful thinking, to suggest that this gentleman was ever near the place.

'The field of the holy men' idea is feasible, but certainly does not refer to the monks of the Blantyre Priory.

The suggestion of a 'promontory' seems a sensible and possible definition, but could also be incorrect, and lacks the romantic touch of 'field of the holy men'.

Rightly or wrongly, I prefer the latter definition, and there is certain evidence to suggest that the holy men were in the district long before 1249 (the suggested date of the founding of Blantyre Priory) and the arrival of the Augustinian canons.

I do not wish to take up any more of your valuable space, but would add that Blantyre, the second largest village in Scotland, after Cambuslang, is an ancient settlement and has afforded me with a fascinating study for a number of years, and has introduced me to a study of the district and of Scottish history in general which I find most rewarding.

I regret to say that the editor thought this letter was too long to publish, and it's not the sort of letter which could be easily cut. So I am glad to publish it now, partly because it tells something of the story of the River Clyde, partly because it shows the difficulties one can get into in writing about the derivation of place names, and mostly because I hold local pride in high regard. Incidentally, if you are in this part of the country, the name of Blantyre is not pronounced to rhyme with motor tyre, but is said, with an even accentuation on each syllable, 'Blan-tirr'.

Since Mr. Smith has quoted the Rev. Stewart Wright's *Annals of Blantyre* and approves of his definition of the name, let me give you what Mr. Wright says.

Blantyre is derived [he wrote in 1885] from the two Gaelic words that signify 'the field of the holy men', for the parish was, to a very large extent, the property of the Church. The first mention of it is in some ancient records, where it is spoken of as belonging to the Abbacy of Jedburgh; the abbot and the monks of which had formed a sort of colony, and here they built their Priory as a 'cell', or retreat for themselves, when compelled to fly from the Borderland during the many bloody wars that raged for centuries between the English and the Scotch. . . .

We cannot tell the exact year when the Priory was built, but we know that it must have been in existence considerably before 1289 [You'll recollect that Mr. Smith, in his letter, says 1249] for there is a mention in one of the old Statute Books of a Prior of Blantyre being present at a Parliament which was held at Briggeham some time during that year; and "Frere William Priour de Blantyre" is likewise alluded to as "a subscriber to Bagimond's Roll" where the Priory is taxed upon a valuation of £66 13s. 4d. This same Prior swore fealty to Edward I of England at Berwick, 28th August 1296.

Prior Walter of Blantyre was one of the Scottish Commissioners appointed to negotiate the ransom of King David Bruce, taken prisoner in the Battle of Durham, in the year 1346.

The last Roman Catholic Prior of Blantyre embraced the principles of the Reformation and became the first Protestant minister of the parish. The name of this worthy man was William Chirnsyde.

When I went to see Blantyre Priory last I was conducted by Mr. William Cunningham, Warden of the Livingstone Memorial, otherwise I doubt if I should have found it. The old pit bings of Blantyreferme Colliery are being taken away, and we had to negotiate fences, hills of mud and other hazards to get to it.

When Hugh Macdonald arrived here in 1854, he recorded in his *Rambles Round Glasgow:*

After a pleasant ramble through the tangled mazes of the wood, we arrived at the Priory, which is situated on a precipitous rock rising to a considerable height above the Clyde. The building, which is of a fine-grained red sandstone, has apparently been at one period of great extent. It is now, however, a complete wreck. A portion of the walls and gables, with several windows and a fireplace, on the verge of the precipice, with a kind of vaulted chamber now threatening to fall in, are all that has been spared by the hand of time. There are several trees growing among the ruins, and the walls are partly covered by the mournful ivy.

Hugh Macdonald saw much more of the priory than I did. Even Mr. Cunnnigham was surprised at how little of the ruin was left since he had been there last. He had heard that the vandals had been at work and saw that the few remaining walls had been thrown into the Clyde below.

There was great excitement in Blantyre a few years ago when someone climbing round the remains of the priory found faces carved in the stone foundations below it. The theory was at once advanced that these had been made by the monks who lived there, but the faces seemed quite modern and the work was not time-weathered. Later a Blantyre youth who was a student at the Glasgow School of Art confessed that the faces were his work. He wanted to practice sculpture and chose this out-of-the-way, not to say dangerous, place to make his carvings.

At one time the priory was the seat of Walter Stuart, who was Lord Privy Seal of Scotland in 1595 and last Commendator of the priory. He was made a peer in 1606 and chose the title of Lord Blantyre. A frequent visitor to the priory was his granddaughter, Frances Stuart, who planted a garden beside Lord Blantyre's orchard. She became Duchess of Richmond and was a great favourite of Charles II, who had her sit as the model for Britannia, used on our coins for so many years.

Romantic people in Victorian days would take visitors to the priory to show them the orchard "planted by Britannia". Today there is no sign of it.

And now we come back once again to Sir William Wallace (and will yet again along the banks of the Clyde). The story goes that, on one of the many occasions when he was hiding from the English soldiers, he asked help at Blantyre Priory. The monks gave him a robe and a cowl and he was able to conceal himself among them. Then they took him to a secret tunnel which ran below the Clyde from the priory to Bothwell Castle on the opposite bank, and so he escaped once more.

It's a great pity that the tunnel does not exist today, because you could take it to the castle instead of going on a most roundabout route to get there. At one time the direct route to Bothwell Castle was simple. If you were following the Clyde from its source, as we are doing, you might go down Blantyre Mill Road to see the Livingstone Memorial, but then you'd come back up to join the main road again. Or, if you were coming from the Glasgow direction, you would go through Uddingston to the main gate of the castle. If we follow our way down the Clyde and return from the Livingstone Memorial, we go along a red sandstone wall and come to a big gate with lodges. That was once the entrance to the castle, but it is now permanently closed.

Now you must go right into Uddingston and follow the signs through the grounds to the castle. Or, if you have been to see the little that remains of Blantyre Priory, you make your way back to the road and go down to the Red Brig and back into Uddingston, avoiding, if possible, the complex of roadways at the new traffic interchange on the other side of the Brig. It's said, by the way, that it's called the Red Brig because a great battle took place here and the Clyde below the bridge ran red with blood. It's a nice story, but I can find no trace of it in history.

It may take you some time to get to Bothwell Castle, but it's worth it. Miss Wordsworth, whom I have quoted already, had a very good description of the castle (and the priory) when she came up the river from the Falls of Clyde:

It was exceedingly delightful to enter thus unexpectedly upon such a beautiful region. [She hadn't thought much of Hamilton and Bothwell.] The castle stands nobly overlooking the Clyde. When we came up to it, I was hurt to see that flower-beds had taken the place of natural overgrowings of the ruin, the scattered stones and wild plants. It is a large and grand pile of red freestone, harmonizing perfectly with the rocks of the river, from which, no doubt, it has been hewn.

When I was a little accustomed to the unnaturalness of a modern garden, I could not help admiring the excessive beauty and luxuriance of some of the plants, particularly the purple-flowered clematis, and a broad-leafed climbing plant without flowers, which scrambled up the castle-wall, along with the ivy, and spread its vine-like branches so lavishly that it seemed to be in its natural situation, and one could not help thinking that, though not self-planted among the ruins of this country, it must somewhere have its native abode in such places.

If Bothwell Castle had not been close to the Douglas mansion, we should have been disgusted with the possessor's miserable conception of adorning such a venerable ruin; but it is so very near to the house that, of necessity, the pleasure-grounds must have extended beyond it, and perhaps the neatness of a shaven lawn and the complete desolation natural to a ruin might have made an unpleasant contrast; and besides, being within the precincts of the pleasure-grounds and so very near to the dwelling of a noble family, it has forfeited, in some degree, its independent majesty and become a tributary to the mansion; its solitude being interrupted, it has no longer the command over the mind in sending it back into past times or excluding the ordinary feelings which we bear about us in daily life.

We had then only to regret that the castle and the house were so near to each other; and it was impossible not to regret it; for the ruin presides in state over the river, far from city or town, as if it might have a peculiar privilege to preserve its memorials of past ages and maintain its own character for centuries to come. We sat upon a bench under the high trees, and had beautiful views of the different reaches of the river, above and below. On the opposite bank, which is finely wooded with elms and other trees, are the remains of a priory built upon a rock; and rock and ruin are so blended that it is impossible to separate the one from the other. Nothing can be more beautiful than the little remnant of this holy place; elm trees (for we were near enough to distinguish them by their branches) grow out of the walls, and overshadow a small but very elegant window.

It can scarcely be conceived what a grace the castle and priory impart to each other; and the river Clyde flows on, smooth and un-ruffled below, seeming to my thoughts more in harmony with the sober and stately images of former times than if it had roared over a rocky channel, forcing its sound upon the ears. It blended gently with the warbling of the smaller birds and the chattering of the larger ones that had made their nests in the ruins.

In this fortress the chief of the English nobility were confined after the battle of Bannockburn. If a man is to be a prisoner, he could scarcely have a more pleasant place to solace his captivity; but I thought that, for close confinement, I should prefer the banks of a lake or the seaside. The greatest charm of a brook or river is in the liberty to pursue it through its windings; you can then take it in whatever mood you like; silent or noisy, sportive or quiet. The beauties of a brook or river must be sought, and the pleasure is in going in search of them; those of a lake or of the sea come to you of themselves.

These rude warriors cared little, perhaps, about either; and yet, if one may judge from the writings of Chaucer, and from the old romances, more interesting passions were connected with natural objects in the days of chivalry than now; though going in search of scenery, as it is called, had not then been thought of. I had previously heard nothing of Bothwell Castle, at least nothing that I remembered; therefore, perhaps my pleasure was greater, compared with what I received elsewhere, than others might feel.

Dorothy Wordsworth gave a description of the ruins of Bothwell Castle that might almost stand today. The Castle itself has changed little since she saw it well over a hundred years ago. Blantyre Priory, as I have said, hardly exists now. On the other hand, the pit bings which formerly disfigured the scene have disappeared or are disappearing. But people who visit Bothwell Castle today may be puzzled by her reference to the Bothwell Mansion.

When the Wordsworths got to Bothwell Castle the owner of the estate was Lord Douglas—the Douglases and the Hamiltons were later united through marriage—and an ancestor of his, the Earl of Forfar, had used the ancient castle as a sort of quarry for stones to build his new castle, later known as the Bothwell Mansion. Nothing remains of the Bothwell Mansion today, though the ancient ruin remains. Incidentally, stones from Bothwell Castle were taken to New York some years ago and made into a rockery there.

Bothwell Castle was built about the year 1242 by Walter Olifard or Oliphant, Sheriff of Lothian. Oliphant is the name generally accepted nowadays, and I shall keep to it. The Oliphants owned it until 1455, when it passed by marriage to the Murrays of Bothwell. Again by marriage it went into the Douglas family. The English Earl of Pembroke held it for various brief periods against Robert the Bruce, but Bruce won. Indeed, at one time there was a keeper of Bothwell Castle who had a notice in the window of his cottage saying, "Bothwell Castle—demolished by R. Bruce, 1337".

King James IV of Scotland eventually gave the castle to Adam Hepburn, who became first Earl of Bothwell. The Bothwell family led the customary up-and-down life of Scottish nobles at that time, but they reached their nadir with James Hepburn, the fourth Earl. This is where we come back to Mary Queen of Scots once again. Although her principal palace was in Edinburgh, and her country was the whole of Scotland, the River Clyde seemed to be the place where the worst of her destiny was worked out.

Mary was wed to Lord Darnley, an effeminate, unscrupulous place-seeker whom she did not love. She had fallen in love with a manly, unscrupulous place-seeker, the fourth Earl of Bothwell. However else they differed, each of them wanted to become King of Scots. Bothwell suggested a divorce to Mary, but this was against her religion. However, early in 1567, Darnley paid a visit to his father in Glasgow and contracted smallpox. He and his wife were at odds, particularly because he had made excuses for not attending the christening of his infant son (later to become James VI of Scotland and I of the United Kingdom) in Stirling Castle.

Nevertheless, Queen Mary, when she heard of her husband's illness, went to Glasgow and sent him her personal physician to look after him. She lived in what is now known as Provand's Lordship in Cathedral Square, Glasgow, and now that it is a museum, you will be shown Queen Mary's room, with furniture and decorations in the style to which she was accustomed. When Darnley was well enough to travel back to Edinburgh, Mary accompanied him. But in the capital their ways parted—Mary to her Palace of Holyroodhouse and Darnley to Kirk o' Field House. He was still ill enough to infect the baby, and that was the reason for their separation.

Despite the danger of infection Mary visited Darnley every day at Kirk o' Field. On the evening of 9th February 1567, she paid one of her visits and explained that she must attend a wedding celebration for two of her servants. She bade him an affectionate farewell, pulling a ring from her finger and placing it on his, and kissing him. Then she went to her party. Later on that night, about two hours after Queen Mary had returned to Holyrood-house, there was a great explosion. Kirk o' Field House had been blown up, but the peculiar thing was that the bodies of Lord Darnley and his servant, who had both been in the house, were found dead in the garden, bearing no signs whatever of having been in an explosion.

The Earl of Bothwell was immediately suspected by his fellow nobles. He was tried on 12th April in Edinburgh, but was acquitted. This may have been because he brought with him to the trial a few friends—in fact, 400 Border lairds and 200 troopers. This kind of persuasion often affected a jury in the old days.

Now Bothwell decided to marry Mary Queen of Scots. He had originally wed a Danish lady, but deserted her on their honeymoon. She is remembered by the old ballad called "Lady Anne Bothwell's Lament", and a song which starts:

> O Bothwell bank, thou bloomest fair,
> But ah! thou mak'st my heart fu' sair!

He became a bigamist when he 'married' Lady Jean Gordon. Then he deserted her and went in for bigamy a second time when he 'married' Queen Mary. Some kind people say that he forced Mary to marry him, but others, not so kind, say that he was the only love of her life and there was no forcing required. At any rate, this was the end, virtually, of Mary Queen of Scots and the Earl of Bothwell.

Bothwell decided to test his right to become King of Scots at the Battle of Carberry Hill. He lost and fled the country. Mary was imprisoned in Lochleven Castle, escaped, went to the Hamiltons on the banks of the Clyde, but was defeated at the Battle of Langside and eventually threw herself on the mercy of the Virgin Queen of England and got her head cut off.

As for Bothwell, he lived a pirate's life for a time on the North Sea and in the Baltic. Perhaps the rest of his life is best summed up by what the guide tells you if you go to see his mummified body in the church of Faarvejle in Denmark. This is one of Denmark's tourist attractions, and the guide explains, "He was a most bad man. First, he plotted to kill Lord Darnley, husband of Mary

Queen of Scots. After Lord Darnley was dead, he dragged her to a marriage ceremony at Dunbar Castle in Scotland. But the Scots did not wish a wicked ruler like that and banished him.

"First he went to Orkney, then to Norway, which we Danes owned. Then he came to Denmark and our king, Frederick II, made him a prisoner. Of course, he pined for his Mary all the time he was in Denmark, and there are those who say he finally died of a broken heart."

There are also those who say he died a raving lunatic. But the man who lived on Bothwell bank is now a shrivelled showpiece in a little Danish town. When the Earl of Bothwell fled the country, Bothwell Castle was given to the Douglas family, and they held it for many years. The last owner, ere it fell into desuetude, was an Earl of Home, who inherited it on the female side of the family. So Bothwell Castle is linked in a way with the 14th Earl of Home who gave up his title so that he could become Prime Minister of Britain.

Bothwell was the 'kirktown' of Bothwell Castle, and it was the place of ceremony for the owners of the castle. The retainers, however, lived in Uddingston, a village built originally by Walter Oliphant to house his servants. You will find it difficult to go along the River Clyde from Bothwell Castle to Uddingston—not impossible, but hardly worth trying. You are better to go through the estate back to Uddingston and continue through that somewhat prosaic little town to Uddingston Station. As you reach the station, you see a path which leads down to the river and to a railway bridge across the Clyde.

As I say, Uddingston looks rather humdrum today, and so I'd like to quote A. G. Williamson, who, in his book, *Twixt Forth and Clyde*, gave a description of the original Uddingston which I cannot better. Here it is:

The town built by Walter Oliphant in the first half of the twelfth century was made entirely of wood, and it was surrounded by a high wooden palisade. This palisade had a ditch on the outside, something after the fashion of a moat. On one side of the road leading up to the town gate was the Common, or burgh moor, a tract of land given to the townspeople by the Baron for the use of their cattle and sheep.

On the other side, that nearer to the palisade, would be the town acres divided into little vegetable plots, one for each householder. The gate had a keeper.

The town consisted of one short main street, with half-a-dozen shorter and narrower lanes breaking off at intervals. The houses were built of wood, and as they were not planned in a straight line many of them butted out on to the middle of the street. The shops were merely booths or carts. The only stone building in the town was the chapel. The centre of the main street was mostly covered with grass, and on this strip of grass cows, goats, sheep and even horses were turned out to browse. Pigs were as common as dogs.

The town refuse was piled up at the sides of the houses and dumped every Sunday morning in a convenient place outside or, failing that, in the cemetery! The flies were as thick as the currants in a fruit cake and the stink atrocious.

As there was no town clock, some poor wretch who could read a sundial was usually commissioned the town drummer. He got up at some unearthly hour, and taking his drum with him, went for a walk through the town to waken the citizens and remind them that it was time they were out of their beds and off to the castle or they would lose their jobs. When the town-herd heard the drum he poked his head out of his bedroom window and blew on his horn to let the beasts know that it was time for them to go out to the burgh moor. At the sound of his horn all the cows, horses, pigs, sheep and goats came sauntering out of the closes on either side of the High Street, and, if the gatekeeper was up and the gate open, they would walk out and down the road to the Common. They were followed by the servants on their way to the castle, and for the remainder of the day the gatekeeper and the town-herd were entirely at the mercy of the women and children.

When night fell and the beasts and men-folk came sauntering back into the town they all went to their beds; for there were no street lamps and the man who could afford to have a candle on his kitchen table was considered one of the "nobs".

The only stir in the town was on market day. On the morning of that day the country people came flocking in with their goods, which they sold or exchanged at the town cross. A fair was held once a year. At this fair there was usually a sprinkling of foreign merchants with bales of brightly coloured cloth and bags of glittering beads for the ladies.

The castle servants had fifty days or seven weeks' holiday with pay. They had barrels of good ale to drink, porridge for breakfast, dinner, tea and supper. The upper class, that is the merchants who fastened lead discs to their scales, or the page who had buried his rival on the refuse dump, could stuff itself with ginger, figs, raisins and almonds, eat rice pudding by the bowlful, dust its venison with pepper, and drink flagons of old wine. This class generally frequented the town prison and paid heavy fines.

I have given this somewhat ironic description of a mediaeval town on the Clyde in full because, apart from the connection with Bothwell Castle, it could have been said of many of the villages and small towns along the banks of the river. Today Uddingston might be described as a town of bakers. Not only is there a big bakery business in Uddingston, but one of the annual local Burns Suppers, held every year about the bard's birthday, 25th January, gives the man who proposes "The immortal memory of Robert Burns" a steak pie to take home with him!

When Lanarkshire was given over mainly to mining, Uddingston became a town of colliers, especially as the famous Blantyreferme pits were just across the river. I have mentioned the lane down by Uddingston Station. I met an old miner there who told me that, at one time, there was a high fence here and a narrow wicket gate. This, he assured me, was to prevent miners who had pinched something big from the pit getting it through. The coal-owners apparently didn't mind pilfering on a small scale, but they had to draw the line somewhere.

He took me down the lane to the bridge over the Clyde. Uddingston miners used this railway bridge in going to and from their work at Blantyreferme. There are new industries on the Blantyreferme site today, and Uddingston workers are still using the bridge. The river upstream looks very fine at this point and my guide pointed out a deep pool which was famous among swimmers.

This, he said, was where the great Miners' Swimming Gala took place in the summer of 1926. That was during the General Strike, when the miners had plenty of time to swim. Thousands lined the banks of the Clyde to see it, and hundreds of swimmers entered for the various competitions. Swimming officials conducted the gala from a raft anchored in the middle of the Clyde, and the highlight of the whole day, according to my friend, was when the raft slowly sank, taking the important officials with it.

On the other side of Uddingston Station there is a charming little suburb of the town running down to the river. Some of the houses have gardens on the bank and the householder can have his own boat. I mention this because, though this is common to many rivers, it hardly ever happens on the River Clyde.

CHAPTER IX

THE RIVER THAT TAM SEATH KNEW

The river that Tam Seath knew? Who's Tam Seath? We know Robert Burns, Sir Walter Scott, David Livingstone, but—we repeat it—who's Tam Seath?

Thomas B. Seath, to give him his proper name, was a shipbuilder at Rutherglen, and his yard was six or seven miles farther up river than the first of the accepted Clyde shipbuilding yards. Indeed, he could only get his ships down to the Firth of Clyde when there was a full tide on the river and he was able to negotiate the weir at Glasgow Green.

We'll come to his full story when we reach Rutherglen along the banks of the Clyde, but perhaps one anecdote will show what manner of man he was. Tam was very small and, like so many small men, rather truculent. On one occasion he was attending a launch at a yard farther down the river when an English shipbuilder, hearing the name of Seath, went up to him and said, "So you're the famous Tam Seath? Why, I could put you in my pocket."

To which the intrepid Tam replied, "In that case ye'd have mair in yer pocket than ye have in yer heid!"

Tam Seath's name is still held in honour along this part of the Clyde, and that is why I dedicate this chapter to him. Indeed, the coat-of-arms of Rutherglen includes two men in a boat, and there are quite a few Rutherglen people who think that this represents some ancestors of Tam Seath. Or, at least, that is what they tell credulous visitors to the Royal Burgh of Rutherglen.

However, we are still in the outskirts of Uddingston and we

can follow the river quite closely down to the Red Brig. One side of the Clyde is farmland. The other, the side we are on, is at the moment a welter of roadways intercrossing at various levels and just as confusing as the traffic interchange between Hamilton and Motherwell. I recall when this seemed the heart of the country a matter of only a few years ago. Up on the main road from Uddingston to Glasgow was a little cluster of houses, not even big enough to be called a clachan, let alone a village, called Old Maryville. There was a narrow country road from the Red Brig to Maryville but it's disappeared in favour of a motorway.

But you can still see what this part of the Clyde looked like before the road developers took over. Keeping to the river you come to the entrance to a Victorian mansion. A legend at the gate says "Greyfriars" and, in fact, the house is occupied (and has been for more than twenty years) by Capuchin Franciscan Friars. Despite the great modern road complex outside, there is an air of tranquillity here, and when you look down at the tree-lined river you expect to see a monk fishing on the banks of the Clyde.

I was shown round the grounds by Father Gilbert, a man with a strong sense of history and a great sense of humour. He pointed out a little island in the river and explained that if there's a good head of water coming down the Clyde this island is submerged. A monk who was new to Greyfriars saw the island on his first day. It rained during the night and the river came rushing down. Next morning the monk went out to survey the scene and came back to announce that the island had been washed away! Although he was reassured that it was still there, he did not believe it until the flow of water abated and the island popped up again.

Just beside Greyfriars a tributary of the Clyde, the North Calder Water, joins the river. Father Gilbert pointed out to me the remains of the foundations of a bridge which once carried the main traffic from London to Glasgow over the Calder. "It was across that bridge," he said, "that Prince Charles Edward Stewart led his Highland army to Glasgow."

This was in 1745, after the retreat from Derby and before the

The Clyde in Glasgow; looking from a Gorbals school across to Glasgow Green

defeat at Culloden. Bonnie Prince Charlie's army followed the Clyde right into Glasgow, but today the river remains more elusive to us.

The stable of Greyfriars has been made into a small and beautiful chapel by the Franciscans, and services are held there every Sunday.

As I have indicated, what Bonnie Prince Charlie could do is, to say the least of it, difficult for us. First of all, there's the problem of crossing the North Calder Water. That means a wide detour and lands you up to the village of Broomhouse and Calderpark Zoo, the zoological gardens of Glasgow and Lanarkshire.

Calderpark was started by some enthusiasts just after World War Two. They could not raise much money—at least, not enough to build big zoological gardens—and at first it was very much a make-do-and-mend affair. It has improved greatly over the years and has gained a certain amount of *réclame* among European zoos for breeding lion cubs.

The Clyde, down by the crematorium and the next-door sewage works, is pastoral at this point, for the last time on both sides. But it's difficult to reach and, at points, dangerous to follow. To get back to the river it's best to go straight ahead and take the red road on the left just as you approach Mount Vernon bridge. This skirts the lands of Kenmuir and takes you to what was once one of the most douce villages on the River Clyde. (Perhaps I should explain that the Scots, because of the Auld Alliance between Scotland and France, use a number of words borrowed, and sometimes bent, from the French. 'Douce' means sweet in French, and that is approximately the meaning in Scots, except that the Scots add a kind of respectability to it!).

This is the village of Carmyle and, though Glasgow Corporation buses run to it, it is still outside the boundaries of the city. Coming down the red road you reach a council housing scheme, and to your left there is some waste ground overlooking the river. On the other side there is an enormous power station in red brick. Across the Clyde is a weir. The weir has been there for many years, but the waste ground was once part of the Kenmuir woods, and a good number of years ago, just as you came in to

8

From Carlton Place there is a view of the Merchants' House steeple and the floating club, the "Carrick"

Carmyle, there was an ornamental fountain with the inscription, "Erected by public subscription to commemorate the vindication of the Kenmuir Right-of-Way by a public demonstration. Saturday, 13th June, 1891."

The fountain has disappeared, as have some picturesque old houses round about what was once a meal mill. It was a sign of democracy that we shall see being repeated as we near Glasgow. The local laird of Daldowie tried to stop the villagers from walking through the Kenmuir woods along the banks of the Clyde, but the Carmylers turned out in force and threw down his walls and fences until he was forced to concede their right to follow the river. He might have done better if he had made the point that the path along the river bank was dangerous. It led to the Marriage Well and so, even if it was dangerous, it was popular.

When I first walked up this way, I passed the fountain and took the path along the bank. I saw the Marriage Well—and admired the scene. But then I found the way so unsafe that I was glad to crawl through a barbed-wire fence and reach the safety of the Daldowie fields. At that time I was writing in my newspaper of my walk up the Clyde, and I knew that readers were, literally, following in my footsteps. So I felt it necessary to warn them that this was a dangerous way.

At that time too, I had not read the words of George Eyre-Todd, the Glasgow historian, on this part of the Clyde:

The old riverside clachan of Carmyle, with its meal mill and its boat house inn, remains yet almost, in the words of the late A. G. Murdoch, "as quaintly rustic as a cuckoo's song". Here the rambler may have pointed out to him the "Bloody Neuk", where, in days gone by, the Damon and Pythias of the region fell in mortal strife over the charms of a fair incomer. And in the river below may be admired the ancient weir with its "scimitar sweep of foam" described a century ago [this was written in 1906] in John Wilson's "Clyde". Thence the path ascends the river bank, past the treacherous sandy "Margin", where many a drowning has taken place, to Kenmuir Wood.

Today the trees have gone, and there is no inducement to take the path to the Marriage Well. You can still admire the weir, but there is no meal mill. But there is still the Auld Boat Hoose, the inn opposite the spot where a boat would ferry people across the Clyde from the Cambuslang side. It looks much the same outside as it did in the days of George Eyre-Todd, but inside it is modern, not to say luxurious, and at the back is a beer garden for the good days in the summer.

The best of Carmyle is along by the Clyde. If you take a road up the hill into the rest of the village, you find yourself in a mixture of villadom and council houses, to say nothing of the aerosol legends on any convenient wall or shed which proclaim that "Carmyle Tahiti Are Mental", and "Carmyle Psycho Are O.K.", or the other way round, of course.

You may have difficulty in believing, unless you keep to the river bank, that Carmyle and Kenmuir were once famous for their attraction for artists. The artists came mainly from Glasgow, and they set up their easels along the Clyde. They included such famous Scottish painters as Horatio McCulloch, Docharty, Sam Bough, McWhirter and George Reid. To see something of what they saw, you must go from the Auld Boat Hoose along past charming little old houses, a pleasant park with elderly trees, a bowling green and a wooded walk. There is a road going up to the right, but you should hold to the path by the Clyde.

You may not find anyone who can point out the 'Bloody Neuk' to you, but you will reach a bridge over the river. The road leads up to Auchenshuggle on the right and to Cambuslang on the left. Straight in front are the great Colville Steelworks and there is a patina of red dust over the whole scene at this point.

If you are very determined indeed you can go straight ahead and follow the Clyde through Colville's works. There are defiant characters, mainly in the city of Glasgow, who regard this walk as a challenge. Indeed, the last time I suggested that, if you were trying to keep to the banks of the Clyde, you would do well to avoid this bit, I was stigmatized as a coward and unworthy of the proud company of river walkers. Well, if you want to slip and shuffle through a kind of slurry of slag overhanging the river, you're welcome to it. To me this is one of the black spots of the Clyde, and I'd rather avoid it. There is, in any case, nothing to see unless you are one of these industrial archaeologists.

The better way to take from here is by Auchenshuggle, but we must first have a look at the largest village in Scotland, Cambuslang. So we turn left at the bridge and climb the hill to Cambuslang. The largest village in Scotland is composed of eight villages stuck together—Kirkhill, Vicarland, East Coats, West Coats, Cullochburn, Bushyhill, Chapelton and Sauchiebog. The only one of these which retains any real identity today is Kirkhill, such an exclusive part of Cambuslang that it doesn't use the village name but sticks to its own.

Of all the places we have visited so far along the banks of the Clyde, Cambuslang has changed more than any other. I can hardly recognize the main street for the place I knew as a boy, travelling in the Glasgow tram-car to the Cambuslang terminus. The centre of the village—it seems quite absurd to describe this town as a village—is half twentieth-century, half nineteenth-century, or perhaps a more accurate proportion might be three-fifths to two-fifths.

I remember going up the road from the Carmyle bridge and finding it still part of the countryside. On the right, near the top of the brae, was a pleasant little house called Rosebank. This was the great David Dale's country mansion. He came here to what he described as "one of the sweetest places on the Clyde" to relax from the rapid pace of Glasgow in the eighteenth century. Actually, he was officially just out of that century, because he bought Rosebank in 1801 and died there in 1806.

David Dale was only following the fashion when he bought Rosebank as a country seat. Many a rich Glasgow merchant decided that Cambuslang was the place to withdraw from the worries of the world. One of them was John More, manager of the Royal Bank of Scotland in Glasgow. He built himself a house at Wellshot at a cost of £17,000. You could multiply that by at least ten to get the cost today. Eventually John More gave up his Glasgow house and settled in Cambuslang. Every afternoon his splendid equipage, complete with black footman, took him from the Bank's office in St. Andrew's Square, Glasgow, to

Cambuslang. And there he lived like a prince until he was found out as an embezzler.

Long, long before the Glasgow merchants settled on Cambuslang as a good place to live, the nobility had had their estates in this airt. Hardly a stone remains of any of the great mansions, but there are still the ruins of Gilbertfield whose laird translated Blind Harry's "Wallace" into more readable Scots. When he read this translation, Robert Burns said, "It poured a tide of Scottish prejudice into my veins which will boil along there till the floodgates of life shut in eternal rest."

Strangely enough, the village is remembered today mainly for that renowned religious revival known as the 'Cambuslang Wark'. The spot where it took place in 1742 is the glen (some people describe it as a 'ravine') of the Kirk Burn, now a park, near Cambuslang Parish Church. The 'Cambuslang Wark' was no Billy Graham affair. It really started by accident. In February 1742 the church was in sad need of repair, and while he was waiting for the necessary funds to put the place to rights the minister, a Mr. McCulloch, held his Sunday services in the ravine, which acted as a sort of sounding board. Mr. McCulloch was the good old sort of minister who referred constantly to his congregation as "hell-deserving sinners".

However, he succeeded in converting two Cambuslang worthies—Ingram More, a shoemaker, and Robert Bowman, a weaver. They were so carried away that they got up a petition asking Mr. McCulloch to give them a lecture every Thursday night, as well as his sermons on the Sabbath. More and Bowman took this petition round Cambuslang and soon got a wheen of signatures.

Mr. McCulloch started his Thursday lectures and, possibly to his surprise, the whole parish turned out to hear them. A kind of exaltation gripped Cambuslang, and the people demanded a lecture every night and not just on Thursdays. The word spread round the country, and soon people were coming from all over the West of Scotland to listen to the preachers at Cambuslang—preachers, because even Mr. McCulloch could not keep up the pace alone and had to call in ecclesiastical helpers.

The 'Cambuslang Wark' lasted for eight months (as far as I know, the longest religious revival ever held), and the climax came with the visit of George Whitefield, the Calvinistic Methodist. At the final sacrament there were 30,000 people present, and Whitefield's resonant voice, backed by the ravine, was said to be heard for miles. Three tents were erected to house those who were overcome by emotion, or any other reason. There were twenty-five tables for the sacrament and 3,000 communicants. On that final day there were 400 converts. To paraphrase a question asked on another Scottish occasion, "Whaur's yer Billy Graham noo?"

Now we go back down the hill to the Clyde. The road crosses the bridge and, as I have said, goes up to Auchenshuggle. Part of Colvilles Steelworks are built on Clyde Ironworks started by the Dunlop family well over 200 years ago. They were built as a 'relief' to the famous Carron Ironworks at Falkirk, and many of the cannon used in the Battle of Waterloo were cast on the banks of the Clyde. The blaze from these ironworks was one of the great Glasgow sights and the 'Radical Poet', Sandy Rodger, wrote some verses about them and about Colin Dunlop, proprietor of the works. One verse will suffice:

> The moon does fu' well when the moon's i' the lift,
> But oh, the loose limmer tak's mony a shift,
> While here, and whiles there, and whiles under a hap—
> But yours is the steady licht, Colin Dulap!
> Na, mair—like true frien'ship—the mirker the nicht
> The mair you let out your vast columns o' licht;
> When sackcloth and sadness the heavens enwrap,
> 'Tis then you're maist kind to us, Colin Dulap!

Apparently being called Colin Dulap did not offend Colin Dunlop at all. He was delighted with the verses and sent Sandy Rodger a five-pound note.

We go up by Colvilles to the main road and Auchenshuggle. This tiny village achieved fame when its name was used as a tram-car terminus by the renowned James Dalrymple, the impresario of the Glasgow cars. Most people thought he had made the name up, because the sight of "Auchenshuggle" on the front of a car made people want to make the journey. But Auchenshuggle is a real place, and the name is a corruption of the Gaelic for 'the field of rye'.

Hardly anything of the original Auchenshuggle remains. A stone shed is pointed out as the schoolmaster's house, and there are one or two very old buildings—or, at least, there were when I was there last. In fact, Auchenshuggle has been swallowed up by Tollcross, an old-enough village in its own right, but not as old as Auchenshuggle. We are now, by the way, within the boundaries of the city of Glasgow, for Tollcross was absorbed by that great octopus in 1912. Tollcross Park was the estate of Colin Dunlop, and he was born in Fullarton House there. So was George Outram, editor of the *Glasgow Herald*. If anyone is interested, I was born just opposite Fullarton House in a red sandstone tenement.

But we are getting away from the River Clyde. If we go along by what was once the Auchenshuggle tram terminus we come to the Roman Catholic convent of Dalbeth and Dalbeth cemetery. At the cemetery there is a lane leading down to the river, and if you follow it to the banks of the Clyde you will be able to walk along them right into the heart of Glasgow. It's a queer mixture of a path, and, strange to say, it's inclined to be more countrylike on the Glasgow side of the river than on the Rutherglen side. For here, right down to Rutherglen Bridge, the right side is in Glasgow and the left bank in the Royal Burgh. The Rutherglen side is full of the works of man, with an occasional breathing space of open country. On the Glasgow side the works of man are better concealed and kept farther back from the Clyde.

The river makes huge loops along this way, and you will find yourself at times walking east instead of west. But every now and then you see the tower of Rutherglen Town Hall.

As you reach the Clyde from Dalbeth you look on the wide and shallow river. It's remarkable to think that grains of gold were found among the sand here many years ago and that there were beds of fresh-water mussels, which sometimes contained pearls. Not so very long ago cattle were grazing in the fields hereabouts, but now most of the farmland is occupied by the bonded warehouses of a firm of whisky distillers. This is appropriate because it was a Glasgow whisky distiller who was the cause of the Battle of Harvie's Dyke in 1822. As you go along the river bank you come to the remnants of a stone wall on either side of the path. This is all that remains of the famous Dyke.

In 1819 Thomas Harvie, distiller, bought the lands of Westthorn at this part of the Clyde. The path along the river was a favourite walk of the weavers from Bridgeton and other parts of the East end of Glasgow, especially on Sundays, and Mr. Harvie decided that this was trespassing. After a year or two he could stand it no longer and had a dyke, or wall, built along his boundary right down to the river, so that the path was closed.

This was more than the independent weavers and other workers could bear. On Saturday, 21st July, 1822 they armed themselves with picks and crowbars and demolished the wall. As they were finishing the demolition the Enniskillen Dragoons were called out, and the ringleaders were arrested. Some of them were sent to prison and Harvie's dyke was rebuilt. But public feeling was aroused, especially by the efforts of the 'Radical Poet' I have referred to already, Sandy Rodger. Some well-known citizens took up the case and started a legal action, which eventually went to the House of Lords. The case was decided against the distiller, and Harvie's Dyke came down again.

This was such a *cause célèbre* that, seven years after the battle, a medal was struck with the inscription, "The Reward of Public Spirit.—The Citizens of Glasgow to Adam Ferrie, Geo. Rogers, Jas. Duncan, Jno. Watson, Junr., Jno. Whitehead, for Successfully Defending Their Right to a Path on the Banks of the Clyde, 1829."

The walk along the Clyde deteriorates hereafter because a long corrugated-iron wall is the river boundary for Belvidere Hospital, one of the first fever hospitals to be built in Britain. The best thing to do is to keep your eyes on the river, for, despite the surroundings, swans glide here and racing boats come up as far as this on training spins. For some time you have been seeing the towers of the Glasgow high flats, but you get a shock when you discover these skyscrapers are actually built on the river bank, with a piazza leading down to the water. And then you are in the wasteland again until you reach Dalmarnock Bridge.

This is the first of fifteen bridges across the River Clyde within the boundaries of Glasgow. It was built in 1889 on the site of an 1821 bridge by the City of Glasgow, the Royal Burgh of Rutherglen and the Lower and Middle Wards of Lanarkshire, and right in the middle of this good Victorian bridge, with its pretty ironwork and marble pillars, are the boundary signs showing the arms of Glasgow on one side and the arms of Rutherglen on the other.

All you have to do is walk across Dalmarnock Bridge and you are in Rutherglen, famous, among many things, for the tongue-twister, "Ru'glen's wee roon' red lums reek briskly". This is a reference to the little, round, red chimneys which poured smoke from the red-tiled roofs of the houses of the Royal Burgh. You will have great difficulty in seeing any examples of them today. One of the last was a little derelict building called 'Ye Olde Inn' with the date 1658 on it. But it has gone in the sweeping changes in the "modernisation" of Rutherglen.

Rutherglen got its royal charter in 1126, and its bounds at one time included part of the ground on which Glasgow now stands. Patriotic Ru'glonians (believe it or not, that's how Rutherglen people describe themselves!) claim that they still own Glasgow. But Glasgow has now taken over Rutherglen under the Strathclyde scheme of redistribution of areas in the West of Scotland. The Ru'glonians, proud and independent, protested strongly. And it is still true that when a Glaswegian enters Rutherglen he knows right away that this is a different place, although the buildings have been more or less contiguous all the way in.

It is said that Rutherglen goes back to pre-Christian times and takes its name from King Reuther, but I trust you will recollect what I said about derivations when I was describing Blantyre. The only really ancient part of Rutherglen is in the grounds of

Rutherglen Old and Greenhill Parish Church on the Main Street. This is the east wall of the 'new kirk' of Rutherglen, built about 1100. It is said that this has been a place of worship since the fourth century, and the first wattle church was built by St. Conval, a disciple of St. Mungo, the patron saint of Glasgow.

Then came the Norman church of St. Mary the Virgin in 1100. It was in this kirk that the Peace Treaty of 1297 was concluded between Scotland and England, a treaty that did not last long. It was here that Sir John Menteith betrayed Sir William Wallace to the English.

There is also a 'Tam o' Shanter'-like tale associated with the old kirk. It's said that the minister of Rutherglen was riding home at midnight when he saw lights shining in the window of the church. He crossed the kirkyard and looked in at a window and, to his horror, saw that a witches' Sabbath was being held. He even recognized members of his own flock clustering around the Devil. This was too much for the holy man and he shouted, "Ye'll no' deny this the morn, ye limmers!"

But out the hellish legion sallied, and before the minister could get to the manse he and his horse were surrounded by witches and warlocks. They cast a spell over horse and man so that neither could stir from the spot until the minister promised never to reveal the names of the people he had seen.

The old kirk was demolished in 1794, and only a little of the building was preserved in the tower. This church lasted until 1900, and the present one was built in 1902. The steeple in the old part is early sixteenth century. The Kirk Port (or gate) was built in 1663, and you can see a sentry box beside it dated 1761. This is a relic of the bad days of the body-snatchers. When a burial had taken place, the relative of the dead person would position himself in the sentry box, fully armed, watching out for night marauders.

Just beside Rutherglen Church is Rutherglen Town Hall, whose tower you have seen so often as you walked around the links of Clyde. It's a piece of 'Scottish baronial' and was built in 1861.

Rutherglen has also a claim to fame in its Main Street, which

is by far the broadest in this part of Scotland. At one time the
Rutherglen market was held here, hence the need for space. This
tree-lined thoroughfare still has atmosphere, but a new centre,
costing £5,000,000, is planned in the same place, together with
a Rutherglen Expressway down by the Clyde. And the wee red
lums will no longer reek briskly, because it will be a smoke-free
zone!

So we cross Dalmarnock Bridge into Glasgow, joining the
river again, and find there is a path of sorts along by the huge
Dalmarnock Power Station. We go under two railway bridges,
and there, on the opposite bank, are the vestiges of the shipbuilding yard of Tam Seath. You can tell the place now only
because there are some yachts and motor boats being repaired—
not by Tam Seath's descendants but by their owners. The fiery
little Tam would explode if he could see what has happened to his
shipyard today. Old Rutherglen Quay also stood there, for there
was a time when Tam Seath ran a small steamer from the weir at
Glasgow Green up the river to the Royal Burgh. This was in 1856,
and it was two years later that he started his shipbuilding yard.

That once-famous Glasgow magazine, *The Bailie*, gave a profile
of Tam Seath in April 1879 and said,

> It will surprise many to learn that Mr. Seath's firm have launched
> over 180 craft from their yard. The steam yachts built by him are
> held in great repute for their graceful modelling, speed, and neat and
> substantial construction. His success in designing and building river
> steamers is amply borne out by such well-known names as the
> *Benmore, Windsor Castle, Bonnie Doon*, &c.

You have to see the River Clyde at this point and realize how
far Rutherglen is up the river to appreciate Tam Seath's genius.
I have voyaged in two of his steamers on the Firth of Clyde, the
Isle of Arran and the *Lucy Ashton*. They were paddlers, and the
Lucy Ashton achieved some sort of macabre after-life because she
was used for testing jet propulsion on water.

These steamers could only be taken down river from Rutherglen when the tide was right, and they could negotiate the weir.
They were pulled by man-power. Any number from forty to

eighty men would line each bank of the river and draw the ship steadily down to deeper water. They used ropes to pull her and restrain her and guide her, and the pilot in charge was a Rutherglen blacksmith who knew every inch of Tam Seath's bit of the Clyde.

As we follow the route of the *Lucy Ashton* down the river, we have Rutherglen still on the opposite bank, and Bridgeton on our own side. Bridgeton was at one time a village of weavers who regarded the Glasgow people as common. Indeed, the village had its own band and, since they always turned out wearing top hats, blue coats and white trousers, they were known as 'The Gentlemen's Band'. But the weaving declined, and when Glasgow took over other industries came in. There came a time when Bridgeton was more famous for its two gangs, the 'Billy Boys' and the 'Norman Conks', than anything else. Except perhaps in the Arabian desert where the sheikhs insisted on getting their head-dresses from Bridgeton.

As far as we are concerned, we notice the detritus of civilization (as someone has called it) along both banks of the Clyde. If you don't know this part of the world but have heard the usual stories of Glasgow, your heart will sink, because you will imagine that the scene gets worse and worse. Prepare for a surprise as you reach Rutherglen Bridge.

Just to keep you in a good mood, someone may point out to you that you are passing the Glasgow Corporation Sewage Works on the way. In fact, a visit to the sewage works is surprisingly pleasant, although it's a bit of a facer when you are offered a glass of the sparkling water as the end product.

Then here is Rutherglen Bridge, built in 1896 and technically not in Rutherglen at all. The boundary between Glasgow and Rutherglen cuts through Shawfield Park, which you see on the other side. This is the headquarters of one of Glasgow's senior football teams, Clyde F.C., and also of a greyhound racing track. Sporting types are fascinated by the fact that a player can kick the ball in Rutherglen and score a goal in Glasgow.

As you reach Rutherglen Bridge you cross the road and gaze down the River Clyde. Apart from a bit of building on your right, it's a sylvan scene. If you have heard that the name Glasgow means 'the dear green place' you begin to wonder if, somehow or other, it's true after all!

CHAPTER X

THE RIVER THAT JAMES WATT KNEW

Once again we stand on a bridge and look down the River Clyde. This time it is Rutherglen Bridge, but we are looking into Glasgow. We have a park on either hand. On the left bank there is Richmond Park, a pleasant place for children (there is often a Punch and Judy show there in the summer), for model yachtsmen—or maybe I should say for men sailing model yachts!— for bowlers, and for people who only want to stand and stare. Behind Richmond Park is Polmadie, and there was once a great saying on this part of the Clyde which went, "Oot o' the warld and intae Polmadie!"

Ere we have a look at it, let me introduce the right bank. Just past the houses Glasgow Green comes into view. From Rutherglen Bridge you walk down some steps on to a path which will lead you right into the middle of the city. And you will be walking by the river all the way, which is a big change from the gyrations and fruitless safaris you may have accomplished in order to see the river from its source. I speak from bitter experience.

Ahead, behind the trees of Richmond Park, are the gleaming towers of the new Gorbals. These high flats are replacing the old Gorbals, the most notorious district of Glasgow. Can any other district in any other town, even including New York, have produced a novel (*No Mean City*), a ballet (*Miracle in the Gorbals*), and a play (*The Gorbals Story*), which said so clearly that this was a dreadful place? Yet it never was such a dreadful place. There were worse districts in Glasgow, let alone comparative areas in other cities. But Gorbals is an evocative not to say euphonious name. Something odd should be happening in a place with a name like the Gorbals.

However, we'll come to the Gorbals in good time. Between Rutherglen Bridge and Glasgow Bridge, in the centre of the city, there are seven other bridges over the Clyde. The pattern of this chapter is to move up the right bank of the river from one bridge to the next, and stop while we consider what is happening to that part of the left bank.

And so we go down the stairs from Rutherglen Bridge and walk by Clydeview Terrace to Glasgow Green itself. A raised piece of stone partly crosses our path, and on the wall opposite is a tablet which announces, "Site of Allan's Pen". This is yet another story of a local laird who tried to stop or hinder the people walking along the banks of the Clyde.

As the eighteenth century turned into the nineteenth a wealthy Glasgow merchant bought the lands of Newhall at this end of Glasgow Green. He built a fine mansion and everything in his garden was lovely, except for one thing. Between his grounds and the lovely Clyde there was a public pathway. He knew he had no right to build across it, but he got the brilliant idea of building over it. And so he had this Pen (or Pend) built from his grounds right down to the river with a tunnel below it for people to walk through. The top of the Pen he had turfed, so that anyone walking across the grass from Newhall Mansion would see no difference in the way down to the Clyde.

The Glaswegians did not like this interference with their rights at all, but they did not take the law into their own hands as the Carmylers did in the case of the Kenmuir right of way and as other Glaswegians did at the Battle of Harvie's Dyke. They simply decided to send Mr. Allan's business to Coventry. A great deal of his business was in cloth woven for him by the hand-loom weavers of Bridgeton. He would supply the material and they did the rest. But now they refused to work for him. Even when he offered increased rates of pay, they continued to boycott him. His business started to suffer.

Then Nature went against Mr. Allan. The winter after Allan's Pen was built, the Clyde came down in flood, carrying great pieces of solid ice. The ice pounded into the Pen and it was reduced to rubble. Mr. Allan might have had his Pen rebuilt, but Fate was also against him. There was a panic in the cotton market and a sudden fall in the price of sugar, and cotton and sugar were the two commodities on which the Allan wealth was built. When he tried to retrieve his fortunes he went deeper into the mud than ever and had to flee to Ireland, where he died in 1809.

Newhall Mansion was sold, but two of Allan's daughters stayed on in a small house in the grounds. One of these ladies had very prominent teeth with artificial metal in them. She was known to the local juvenile delinquents as 'Jenny wi' the iron teeth'. They might shout this after her in broad daylight, but when night fell they were sure that she was a witch and wouldn't go near the neglected and overgrown estate.

At the end of the nineteenth century Newhall mansion was demolished, and a letter appeared in a Glasgow newspaper purporting to be from some relative of the notorious Mr. Allan. It suggested that a tablet should be erected at the riverside to commemorate Allan's Pen. As James Cowan says in *From Glasgow's Treasure Chest*,

> In view of all the circumstances, it seems strange that anyone should consider either the Pen or its builder worthy of a memorial stone; but there it is, and whether or not it is worth remembering, Allan's Pen will not be forgotten as long as that stone remains in position.

We reach Glasgow Green and see long lines of football pitches stretching towards trees in the distance. In this area coal was discovered just about the time of Allan's Pen. But shafts could not be sunk because river mud kept filling them up. How grateful Glaswegians must be to the Clyde, for the mind boggles at a group of coal mines in the heart of the city.

A pleasant path runs by the river, and hereabouts was Arn's Well, one of several which, in early days, supplied water to Glaswegians. The time came when Glasgow Town Council had the remarkable idea of piping water from Loch Katrine into the very houses. This great step forward was not popular in some

The Clyde as it flows through the centre of Glasgow

quarters. The criticism was best expressed by an old lady from Bridgeton who had the water supply put into her house but would never turn on a tap. When she needed water, she took a couple of pails to Arn's Well because she said, "This new water has neither taste nor smell!"

A good deal of boating goes on hereabouts on the Clyde, and at one time an abortive attempt was made to start a canoeing centre. But most of the boats you see on this part of the river are racing craft from the clubs a little lower down the Clyde.

Now we reach a somewhat functional-looking cement bridge, which is known throughout the areas on both sides of the Clyde, as the 'Unlucky Brig'. It is for pedestrians only and has replaced a wooden structure, which was, of course, the first 'Unlucky Brig'. I have been unable to discover how these bridges got this name. The purpose of a bridge here is to allow the workers on the right bank access to industry on the south bank, because there have always been factories and works in the Polmadie area.

The other side of the river, from Rutherglen Bridge to the Unlucky Brig, is particularly attractive. The background is the pleasant Richmond Park, but there is a path by the river outside the park railings, and here willows grow athwart the stream, and on a night when there is a fine sunset you look across Glasgow Green to the steeples and towers and skyscrapers of the city, and the scene looks not unlike some of these fine engravings of Glasgow by Joseph Swan and his like, which are so expensive today.

Behind Richmond Park, as I have said, is Polmadie, and the great Glasgow legend is that it got its name when Mary Queen of Scots was escaping from the defeat of her army at the Battle of Langside. She was riding a horse named Poll and, as she was crossing the burn known as Mall's Myre (or sometimes Jenny's Burn), the horse slipped and broke a leg and had to be destroyed. Mary is said to have exclaimed sadly, "Poll may dee that I may live!"

This is a very nice story, spoiled only by the fact that the district was called Polmadie long before Mary Queen of Scots was

9

Sailing ships still visit the Port of Glasgow

born. According to some experts, Polmadie comes from the Gaelic and means 'the pool of the wolves'.

We don't have to believe this legend, but we can see Mall's Myre. It runs in a little ravine through Richmond Park into the Clyde just above the Unlucky Brig. In full flood it's quite pleasant, but during a hot spell in the summer it's not much more than a stinking ditch.

Now we return over the Unlucky Brig and see before us the Fleshers' Haugh on the right bank. It is part of the great area of football pitches which we have already seen. The Fleshers' Haugh has always been a place for demonstrations in Glasgow, though its last demonstration must be well over a hundred years ago. The biggest demonstration was organized by Bonnie Prince Charlie towards the end of 1745. As we learned at Greyfriars he was leading his Highland Army back from Derby, and he knew that the city of Glasgow was anti-Jacobite.

He had to make a show of force to cow the people of Glasgow, and so, it is said, he marched his Highlanders in from the East along the Trongate, above the Clyde, took them round a back road and marched them through again. He did this three times, so that the Glaswegians, who could not tell one Highland warrior from another, thought his army was three times bigger than it really was!

He thought of giving the city over to fire and rapine, but Cameron of Lochiel interceded on behalf of the inhabitants and the prince took money, clothes and shoes instead, enough to re-equip his army. Because of his intercession, the descendants of Cameron of Lochiel are greeted with a peal of bells from the Tolbooth Steeple at Glasgow Cross, and it's not long ago that the present Chief of the Camerons went to the cross and heard the bells played in honour of his ancestor.

Before he withdrew his army from Glasgow, Bonnie Prince Charlie reviewed his men on the Fleshers' Haugh overlooking the Clyde. There was a very small audience for this review, because most Glaswegians looked the other way when Charles or his men were about. But there was a small group of ladies who thought Prince Charles was wonderful, and among them was a young girl called Clementina Walkinshaw, the daughter of a Glasgow laird. The time was to come when she would leave Glasgow and follow the exiled prince wherever he might go throughout Europe. She bore him a child but he never married her.

I remember a time when the Annual Glasgow Police review took place on the Fleshers' Haugh, but the only reminder of those days is when you see a troop of Glasgow Mounted Police come cantering through the morning mist on an exercise round the football fields. The Fleshers' Haugh is also used for the annual Glasgow Fair, a big carnival held in July, and it has been the site of various visiting circuses in its day.

Now we reach King's Bridge, built in 1933, a fine affair in gleaming granite but lacking something in character. It is built over the site of the Oatlands Ferry. On the other side of the bridge three Covenanters were killed at the ferry edge by the Government dragoons in 1685. This district was known as Little Govan then.

From the Unlucky Brig to the King's Bridge on the other side is not as pleasant as it has been up till now. The parkland is replaced by not very prepossessing tenements coming down almost to the water's edge. Behind them are more skyscrapers, loosely identified with the Gorbals but actually outside that district. It's a strange thing that almost all the way down the river from its very source the right bank is usually more interesting than the left bank. We have found it so up till now. We shall find it increasingly so right down to the Firth of Clyde itself.

From the King's Bridge it's but a short step to the St. Andrew's Suspension Bridge, but it gives us a chance to look over the part of Glasgow Green which James Watt knew. The great inventor knew the River Clyde well but, since he lived not far from Glasgow Green, this was the part he knew best. Indeed, it was when he was walking across the Green one Sunday afternoon that he got his idea for the use of the condensation of steam. In my childhood days we were taught that James Watt, sitting by the kitchen range, saw the lid of his mother's kettle lifting with steam pressure and so got his great idea. I even remember a picture showing this very scene.

Like so much that we are told in childhood, this was nonsense. Watt himself has said that the idea came to him on Glasgow Green, though it must have been germinating for some time before that. It's interesting to note that, according to the manners of the time, James Watt had no business to be walking across Glasgow Green on the Sabbath. The strict rules were that people should not be out on a Sunday unless they were walking to or from the kirk. If Watt had been caught on that Sunday, he would have been fined, if not imprisoned. That might have sent his ideas about steam engines out of his head for evermore!

Glasgow Green is the oldest public park in Britain. We have to be careful about our definitions here. The famous parks in the centre of London—Hyde Park, Kensington Gardens, St. James's, the Green Park—are old, but these were all royal parks and the ordinary folk were not allowed in. Glasgow Green was already a public park in the sixteenth century. It should be said, by the way, that Glasgow has more parks per head of population than any other town in the world. There are sixty-two main parks and something like 200 smaller parks and recreational spaces.

In James Watt's days Glasgow Green was not only a place where the people of the town loved to saunter on good days. It was also Glasgow's first golf course. And it was famous for its washing greens, where handsome young women, with their skirts tied up about their waists, trampled the washing in tubs called boynes. This inspired an eighteenth-century Glasgow poet, John Mayne, to write:

> Whae'er has daunnered out at e'en,
> And see the sights that I hae seen,
> For strappin' lasses tight and clean,
>   May proudly tell
> That, search the country, Glasgow Green
>   Will bear the bell.

Down from the King's Bridge we come to the first section of boating clubs' headquarters. Here, in one building, you can find the Glasgow Schools' Rowing Club, the Glasgow Printing Trades Amateur R.C., the City of Glasgow Amateur R.C., the Glasgow Argonauts Boat Club and the Glasgow University Boat Club.

Rowing on the River Clyde is a very democratic affair, and the university is in the minority, although it will be bolstered by the new University of Strathclyde and other colleges in the city. Glasgow rowing clubs have done extremely well in international contests, and the school clubs have been particularly notable in this respect.

We have reached the elegant St. Andrew's Suspension Bridge, which, like the Unlucky Brig, was erected to take workers from one side of the Clyde to the other, and I must depart from my practice so far of following the left bank after we've discovered the right bank. The left bank is drably industrial thereabouts, and we are better to stay put, rather than investigate drabness.

We have come to the most interesting part of Glasgow Green. From the suspension bridge, we see, below us on the right, the landing stage for the boat-hirer, Benjamin Parsonage, Jr. When I visited it the last time there were thirty small boats for hire. But hiring boats is not really Benjamin Parsonage's job. He occupies the handsome house just above the boat-hiring place and is the representative of the Glasgow Humane Society. In other words, he looks after rescues in the river and is also involved in trying to find the bodies of drowned people. The name of Parsonage is highly regarded in Glasgow and Benjamin has done this work since he became assistant to the renowned Geordie Geddes in 1928. (One of the famous lines in Glasgow pantomines when things got a bit rough was "Send for Geordie Geddes!") Benjamin Parsonage took over from Geordie in 1932.

Looking across the green we see several Glasgow landmarks. The first is a replica of the Doge's Palace in Venice. It is, actually, Templeton's Carpet Factory, and there is an addition in the same vein beside the original building. Templeton's are one of the biggest carpet makers in the world. They have made golden carpets for several Coronations in Westminster Abbey. They make carpets for great occasions everywhere. They also make carpets for ordinary homes in Glasgow.

I recollect an occasion when I was asked to take a Russian journalist, a Mr. Agapov of the *Moscow Literary Review* round Glasgow on a Saturday morning. I had already been in Moscow myself, and when I got to Red Square and saw the Kremlin I was strongly reminded of Templeton's Carpet Factory beside the Clyde. This is only natural. A good deal of the Kremlin, but particularly the walls with their fish-tailed battlements, was designed by an Italian architect of the same period as the Doge's Palace. So you get the same architectural features in the Kremlin as you get on the carpet factory.

So I took Mr. Agapov into Glasgow Green, and here I am going to anticipate our journey down the river. We went in to the Green through the flowers and the trees and came to the Doulton Fountain. This is the only relic left in Glasgow of the city's first famous exhibition of 1888 in the Kelvingrove Park. Glasgow has always been famous for its Exhibitions, but this was the first. The English firm of Doulton erected a fountain in honour of Queen Victoria, and so it is, as can well be imagined, an epitome of everything Victorian.

I was pretty certain that Mr. Agapov would like this, because what had struck me more than anything else on my first visit to the Soviet Union was that the Russians were very Victorian in outlook. I was right in the case of Mr. Agapov. The Doulton Fountain, with its effigy of the Queen and the representatives of her Empire, struck him all of a heap. He took no fewer than thirty-four pictures of the fountain. I know that that figure is correct: I counted them. Since then, vandals have struck.

We walked on through the trees to the Nelson Monument on Glasgow Green. This monument in the style of Cleopatra's Needle was the first to be erected in honour of Admiral Lord Nelson. In 1806, long before any of his fellow countrymen commemorated Nelson in stone, the Glaswegians put up this memorial. Technically, it was not the first, however. After word of Nelson's victory at Trafalgar reached Scotland, some English ironworkers at Taynuilt on Loch Etive pulled a boulder into the centre of the village and inscribed a tribute to Nelson on it. It can still be seen behind the parish kirk.

Glasgow Town Council had no hesitation in agreeing to put up the Nelson Monument. But one of the bailies, a man of a practical turn of mind, thought the monument could have a practical as

well as a historical value. Some twelve miles from Glasgow is a
town named Neilston, pronounced "Nelson" in the West of
Scotland. The bailie suggested, therefore, that under the name
"Nelson" there should be carved "12 Miles"!

I did not tell Mr. Agapov this story, because I felt that it would
be difficult to translate. But I pointed out that this was (or has
been, for it's not so popular nowadays) Glasgow's equivalent of
the Speakers' Corner in Hyde Park.

We walked on by the People's Palace and the Winter Garden.
The People's Palace is one of Glasgow's museums and houses the
Old Glasgow collection as well as a remarkable tribute to Sir
Thomas Lipton, the Glasgow grocer who became a friend of the
mighty because of his attempts to bring back the 'America Cup'
to this country. Many of the trophies he won with his yachts are
displayed in the People's Palace. There is also an organ made by
James Watt and still playable to this day.

Beyond the People's Palace we came to the Italian-cum-
Kremlin walls of Templeton's Carpet Factory, and all I can say is
that Mr. Agapov felt just as much at home as I did in Red Square.
And when he looked across to the other side of the Clyde he saw
onion towers and minarets that looked still more like Moscow.
Actually, it's an enormous bakery, and the architect designed it
deliberately to complement the Doge's Palace on the right bank.

Now that we're across St. Andrew's Suspension Bridge, let's
stay there until we reach Albert Bridge, though we have not
finished yet with the right bank by any means. However, it's
more convenient to go this way at the moment. We walk from a
factory area into the new Gorbals, a series of shimmering skyscrapers interspersed with lower buildings and still including (at
the time of writing, at any rate) some of the old slums which made
the name of Gorbals a byword. Indeed, Alexander McArthur, the
author of *No Mean City*, lived here, but the tenement in which he
had a 'single-end' (a one-roomed flat) has disappeared. A bitterly-
disappointed man, he decided to commit suicide by swallowing
poison and throwing himself into the Clyde at this point. But the
poison was too much for him, and he was found dying on the
bank of the river.

The towering new buildings end with a new school, with terraces reaching down to the Clyde and a jetty from which the pupils can embark for sailing lessons. Appropriately, just across the way is the ultra-modern building of the new College of Nautical Science. There is still much to be done in cleaning up the Gorbals, but it is only a matter of a year or two ere it lives up to Sir Basil Spence's design for it.

Now we have reached the Albert Bridge over the Clyde, so we must return to the right bank, where we diverged at the Doge's Palace. I have described, via Tovarich Agapov's visit, what lies between the river and the houses to the north. But you can still walk along by the Clyde, past the once popular and now little used bandstand, the allotments which are a relic of two World Wars, and up by another boating building, where the Glasgow Schools Rowing Club, the Clyde Amateur Rowing Club, and the Clydesdale Amateur Rowing Club have their headquarters and their boats.

There is an aqueduct over the weir, and between it and the Albert Bridge there is what appears to be an outlet for a sewer. This is the fate of the famous Molendinar Burn, the real source of Glasgow's greatness. The Molendinar rises some miles to the North-East, from Hogganfield Loch, and was once a pellucid stream on the banks of which the first Glaswegian, St. Mungo, built his cell in the sixth century and started the ecclesiastical community from which Glasgow developed.

The Molendinar can still be seen, here and there, in the city, but it is even more elusive than the Clyde. Most of it was turned into a sewer by our thoughtful Victorian ancestors, and they joined some other notable streams, including the Camlachie Burn, to the Molendinar to make it an even bigger and better sewer. In old prints of Glasgow you can see the Molendinar running sweetly down by the Cathedral, but the Victorians built a street over it and called it Wishart Street in honour of one of Glasgow's Bishops.

We walk up, over the hidden Molendinar, to the entrance to Glasgow Green and across the Saltmarket (or what is called Jocelyn Square) we see the High Court of Glasgow. Before it was the High Court it was the site of the Glasgow prison, and here, between the two pillars of the entrance, felons were hanged in public. There is an old saying in the East End of Glasgow: "You'll die facing the Monument!" That is an insult, because when a man who was going to be hanged mounted the scaffold between the pillars the last thing he saw before the hangman put the hood over his head was the Nelson Monument on Glasgow Green. So "You'll die facing the Monument!" means that you're going to be hanged.

The last man to be hanged in public at this square beside the Clyde was Dr. Edward William Pritchard, known as 'Pritchard the poisoner' and 'The Human Crocodile', because he wept crocodile tears over his wife and his mother-in-law, the two women he murdered. He was hanged on a summer's day in 1865, and an enormous crowd (estimated variously at 30,000 and 80,000) turned out to see him being turned off.

Dr. Pritchard had his practice in fashionable Sauchiehall Street. He was English, tall, bearded and always well dressed. Other doctors were doubtful about his medical attainments, but he was a popular man in Glasgow and well known for his lectures. Indeed, he gave the very first lecture in the Rutherglen Town Hall we have seen so often from this part of the Clyde.

When he went to be hanged he dressed for the occasion. He wore his best coat and trousers and a new pair of patent leather boots. When he had been hanged, he was buried with other murderers in a piece of unconsecrated ground just beside the prison.

The prison was pulled down and the High Court took its place. But the plot of murderers' graves was left untouched, until the authorities decided that Glasgow needed a mortuary. A firm of plumbers was employed to lay the pipes in this very piece of ground, and soon the workmen were coming across skeletons. One skeleton was that of Dr. Pritchard. They could tell it was the doctor because the initials "E.W.P." were carved on a small headstone. And they discovered that Dr. Pritchard's patent leather boots were still in a perfect state of preservation. The footwear disappeared, and it's thought that, for some time, somebody was going about Glasgow in Dr. Pritchard's boots!

In Dr. Pritchard's day (and in mine too) this was known as Jail Square. It was changed to Jocelyn not only because there was no longer a jail there, but also in honour of the Archbishop who gave Glasgow its annual fair, held in the middle of July. This is appropriate because the Glasgow Fair was held between the High Court and the entrance to Glasgow Green. Here were the shows, the circuses, the tents, the stalls and even wooden theatres which could accommodate audiences of up to 5,000. Nowadays the fair is held, as I have mentioned, on the Fleshers' Haugh and, judging by old prints, is but a shadow of its former self, although big enough by today's standards.

And now we are at the Albert Bridge, named, naturally, after the Prince Consort. It must be remembered that the Clyde is a most volatile river. We have left St. Andrew's Suspension Bridge, built in 1856. Before that there was a ferry across the river at this point, but it was dangerous in time of spate. So the suspension bridge was built for the factory workers and the ferry service came to an end.

The Albert Bridge, a way into Hutchesontown in the eighteenth century, was completed in 1795. A few months later it was swept away by flood. A second bridge was built here in 1829, but it was replaced in 1871 by the present bridge. On the bridge there is a large plaque of Prince Albert, Queen Victoria with a gilded crown, various coats-of-arms and other decorations. There is a tablet which records that the foundation stone was laid by the Grand Master Mason of Scotland, the Earl of Dalhousie, in 1870.

There's no doubt at all that this was considered a very important bridge. It's by far the most decorated bridge, in the way of plaques and legends and announcements, on the whole River Clyde. I have given only a few. If you want to know the names of the architects, the contractors, the justices of the peace, the trustees, Old Uncle Tom Cobley and All, you'll find them in stone print on or about the Albert Bridge.

Once again we stand on a bridge and look down the river. It's a very short view, because directly in front of us is the railway bridge leading into the long abandoned St. Enoch Station.

Nothing goes over this bridge. The station itself is a car park. Fortunately, the St. Enoch Hotel is still there. I suppose the time will come when the St. Enoch Bridge is removed. It will be no great loss.

On the right bank there is the south side of the High Court buildings. If you look carefully, you will see a much-weathered legend stating that the height of the River Clyde rose to this mark in the great flood of—and the date is obliterated. The fact is that there was a series of great floods in the nineteenth century and this was one of them.

Just before you reach the Victorian castellations of the railway bridge you see a narrow way named Old Shipbank Lane. If you go up this lane you will find yourself in Paddy's Market.

Up at the top of the Saltmarket (originally the market for salt to 'cure' salmon) is Glasgow Cross, the traditional centre of the city, dominated by the Tolbooth Steeple, built in 1626. When Daniel Defoe came this way in the eighteenth century, he was so impressed that he described Glasgow as "the most beautiful little city in Britain".

Although you go down from Glasgow Cross along the Saltmarket to the Albert Bridge over the Clyde today, that's not the original route. In Defoe's day you would go down the Saltmarket as far as the Bridgegate (known locally as 'the Briggait') and turn along it to join Stockwell Street, which would lead you to Glasgow's oldest bridge.

At the corner of the Saltmarket and the Briggait stood Glasgow's first bank, the Ship Bank. It is commemorated today by a pub at that very corner, and on each window of the pub is engraved a representation of what the corner looked like when the Ship Bank stood there. The Ship Bank was later merged with the Thistle Bank, and, in turn, they became the Union Bank of Scotland. Then the Union Bank was taken over by the Bank of Scotland. The interesting point is that the original insignia of the Ship Bank, a ship in full sail, has been used on every different bank note of the mergers since the first one with the Thistle Bank, and is still to be seen on the new Bank of Scotland notes.

In the eighteenth century the Briggait was the centre of fashion in Glasgow. It was lined by the mansions of the rich Glasgow merchants, and at the Stockwell Street end stood the Merchants' House, built in the middle of the seventeenth century, and the place where the great balls and assemblies of Glasgow were held. On a winter's night in the Briggait the street would be alive with torches as brawny Highlanders carried the leading ladies of the town in sedan chairs to the Merchants' House.

The glory departed from the Briggait. The rich merchants built houses in what they considered the 'country', far outside Glasgow. Some of these mansions are considered to be in the city centre nowadays, but early Glaswegians were certain that the city would move east. They built their houses in the west and were soon overtaken by the spreading town.

From being a fashionable centre, the Briggait went down and down. By the early nineteenth century it was only half inhabited. Tall houses, once occupied by the gentry, stood empty. This desuetude coincided with the Hungry Forties, the time of the terrible Potato Famine in Ireland (and famine elsewhere, including the Highlands of Scotland). If an Irishman had any money, he took his family to America. If he had had a little money, he went to Liverpool. If he had no money, he came to Glasgow.

It cost the Irish fourpence per skull (an appropriate word, as I shall explain in a moment) to sail from Belfast, up the Clyde to the Broomielaw, then Glasgow's only harbour. Sometimes a ship full of Irish people coming into Scotland passed in the Firth of Clyde a ship full of Highlanders leaving Scotland, usually for Canada. The voyage from Belfast to the Broomielaw took a minimum of thirty hours, and the Irish were packed into the ship like herring in a barrel. They had to stand shoulder to shoulder for the whole thirty hours and sometimes, when the ship docked at the Broomielaw, it was discovered that some of the immigrants had died standing up.

The Irish came up the Clyde with little more than the clothes they were wearing. The Glaswegians rallied to their aid. They started soup kitchens and invented jobs and did all they could to look after poor, starving people. Housing was a big problem, but a number of the immigrants solved that for themselves by moving into the big empty houses in the Briggait. They were probably Glasgow's first 'squatters'.

A common sight in the Briggait in those bad old days was an Irishman standing shivering in the gutter while he held out a shirt for sale. The shirt was his only one, which he had taken off his back, and he was trying to sell it to keep his family alive.

And that is the origin, some 130 years ago, of 'Paddy's Market', down Old Shipbank Lane, between the Briggait and the Clyde. You may still see someone holding out a shirt for sale. But it's not a shirt he's taken off his own back. It's more likely to be one which has been pinched from a clothes-line somewhere. One of these days, though, 'Paddy's Market' may disappear entirely.

We have gone down Old Shipbank Lane and are at the riverside once more. Just across Clyde Street, where railings stand at the grassy edge of the river, there is the famous Cat Ladder. Nobody knows when this Cat Ladder was first put up, but the legend is that a Victorian lady was disturbed at the number of stray cats she saw on this bank of the river, mewing piteously because they could not get back up to the street. Accordingly, she had a ladder built, running from the grass up to street level, and soon the local cats were using it both ways. Every time the Cat Ladder looks like falling to bits, some other animal lover comes along and has it repaired or renewed.

Under St. Enoch railway bridge we come to the Glasgow Fish Market, an elaborately ornamented grey building in the Victorian style, with the seventeenth-century steeple of the old Merchants' House still standing up in the middle. When the Tobacco Lords of Glasgow were controlling most of Europe's supplies of tobacco from America, they would frequently climb this steeple to the observation post at the top to see if their ship or ships had come in at the Broomielaw.

The view down the river is blocked by bridges now, but anyone who climbed to the top tower of the four which make up the Merchants' House steeple will still see a ship. Just on the other side of the Victoria Bridge a clipper ship is moored. It was originally the sailing vessel *City of Adelaide*, built at Sunderland in 1864 and a contemporary of the renowned *Cutty Sark*. Now it is the S.V.

Carrick and headquarters of the R.N.V.R. Club (Scotland)—and carries a television aerial at her masthead!

The Briggait has come down to join Stockwell Street just before it reaches Victoria Bridge, which occupies the site of Glasgow's very first bridge over the Clyde. This was the site of the little salmon fishing village which existed in St. Mungo's day. As I have said, Glasgow began where the cathedral is now, and it moved down the line of what is now the High Street to Glasgow Cross, and then by the Saltmarket and the Briggait to the fishing village.

This was in comparatively modern times, of course—the middle of the sixth century. Much earlier the Clyde ceased to be a river about Rutherglen and became a wide estuary. We can tell this because sand still exists over a wide area on both sides of the river. The great shopping centre of Argyle Street, which has the biggest stores in the city, is built on sand. And when the foundations of the City Chambers in George Square were being dug, the remains of prehistoric canoes were found in the sand there.

But the geological changes which have given Glasgow so many hills (at one time, when the city was smaller than it is now, it had sixteen Hill Streets!) closed the river in and made it the narrow water it is today. Instead of the river ending at Rutherglen, it now runs as far as Dumbarton before it begins to widen into the Firth of Clyde.

From the sixth century there seems to have been a ford at this point in the river, and no one knows when the first attempt at a bridge was made. According to Blind Harry, the poetic chronicler of the Scottish War of Independence, Sir William Wallace crossed the Clyde here by a "brig of tree", which would indicate some kind of wooden structure. But the first Glasgow Bridge proper was that built, again at this point, by Bishop Rae from the cathedral on the hill above the north bank and Lady Lochow, who owned the ground on the south bank. This was in 1345, and the bridge, of eight piers and a mere twelve feet in width, was built of stone. It was widened twice and it lasted for more than 400 years.

Strange to say, when you consider the plethora of plaques and emblems on the Albert Bridge not so very far away, there is nothing on the Victoria Bridge to show that it is on the site of the first Glasgow Bridge, the only one of any importance to cross the whole River Clyde from source to sea. It was across this same bridge, built in 1345, that the Regent Moray rode to the Battle of Langside in 1568 to defeat Mary Queen of Scots. And Bonnie Prince Charlie may have crossed it in 1745, because it was not replaced by a new bridge until 1768.

The present bridge is still the oldest in Glasgow. The foundation stone was laid by the Duke of Atholl in 1851. Like the Albert Bridge, it crosses the Clyde into the Gorbals. But we shall keep to the right first of all.

Stockwell Street, leading from the Trongate-Glassford Street crossing to the Victoria Bridge, does not seem a glamorous sort of thoroughfare. Nevertheless, it is said to owe its name to yet another exploit of the indefatigable William Wallace. At one time the Ratton Well stood here, but Glaswegians seldom used the water because of the impurities in it. The story was that Sir William and his men had a skirmish with English troops around this airt and when, as usual, the Sassenachs were defeated, the Scots threw the dead bodies into this well. Wallace stood by, shouting, "Stock it well, lads—stock it well!" Hence Stockwell Street.

The Ratton Well has long since gone, but visitors are still intrigued by the odd name of a lane which runs round from the Fish Market called the Goosedubs. 'Dubs' is the Scottish word for puddles of water, and the lane got its name from the fact that a Glasgow magistrate had a house here and kept geese which paddled about in the puddles.

The skeleton of the burnt-out Metropole Theatre is across the way. It was once the Scotia Music Hall, the oldest music hall in Scotland, where such giants of the past as the Great Leybourne, Cissie Loftus, Charlie Coburn and Harry Lauder appeared. The story is that when Harry, as a very young man, made his first professional appearance here, Mrs. Baylis, the formidable proprietrix of the Scotia, paid him his money and said, "Noo sonny, awa' hame and practise!" The Metropole Theatre would have been rebuilt if it had not been for the river sand below it. The cost today was too much for the people who owned it.

Not far up is a plaque marking the place where James McGill, the founder of McGill University, Canada, was born in 1744. Opposite there is a building, now a warehouse, which was once the fashionable hotel in which the immortal Jenny Lind was a guest when she was taking Glasgow by storm. Yes, Stockwell Street is typical of the older parts of Glasgow. It may not look much—unless it is seen through the eyes of love.

From Stockwell Street we walk along Clyde Street and see the start of a great new scheme to beautify the banks of the river. It covers the stretch from Victoria Bridge to Glasgow Bridge and is built as a handsome promenade with cafes, shops, a bandstand and other amenities. It will finish up as part of a facelift in the middle of the city. Glasgow Town Council organised a competition for ideas to develop this river area. There is a first prize of £10,000 and a total prize-list of £23,000.

If, instead of walking along the new promenade, we keep to the pavement on the city side of the Clyde, we arrive at a glass warehouse—I should say, a warehouse which sells glass! If you go into the showroom, you're surprised to see the entrance to a house, pillars, steps and all. This was the front door of the Dreghorn mansion in the eighteenth century. The Dreghorns were rich Glasgow merchants (and, as I have indicated, rich Glasgow merchants were *very* rich), but the line ended with Robert Dreghorn, known to the Glasgow gossips as 'Bob Dragon', the ugliest man in the city.

This was Bob Dragon's town house. He also had a mansion far outside Glasgow at Ruchill—which is now well inside the city boundary. I quote George Eyre-Todd, the Glasgow historian on Robert Dreghorn, alias Bob Dragon:

Though the ugliest man in town, with inbent back, huge head, a single eye which squinted, and an acquiline nose bent almost flat to his face, he spent his time in following the best-looking women he could see about the streets. After he died, by his own hand, in this house in 1806, it was said to be haunted. . . .

In the notorious times of Burke and Hare, the body-snatchers, the Dreghorn mansion in Clyde Street was bought by a newcomer to Glasgow who, like most newcomers, was regarded with suspicion. Although Burke and Hare were practising their art in Edinburgh, there were plenty of 'sack-'em-up men' in the West of Scotland too, and every Glasgow graveyard had its armed watchers making sure that the coffins remained undisturbed.

In the middle of the nineteenth century the part of the city running from this point up to the Trongate and around the Gallowgate was largely a slum such as the worst slums seen today would seem like a garden suburb. The slum dwellings were in wynds and closes and were often fronted by most respectable houses and churches and official buildings.

Word went round the slums that several people looking down through the basement windows of the Dreghorn house had seen severed human heads weltering in their gore. This was taken to mean that the new owner of the house was a 'burker' or body-snatcher. The mob gathered and attacked the mansion. They broke in and sacked the place and lit fires—though they found no bodies, not even severed heads.

The situation was too much for the embryonic police force of the time, and a daring Glasgow magistrate rode across the bridge to Port Eglinton, where the dragoons were quartered. He rode back to the Clydeside at the head of the horsemen and the mob were quickly brought under control. Some of the arrested leaders were flogged through the town, the last time that this sentence was carried out in Glasgow.

It is quite amazing to stand in this douce Glasgow ware-house, with people on all sides buying glasses and crystal and ornaments, and reflect on the cruel fate of Bob Dragon and the savagery of the mob attack on this very portal in front of your eyes.

We leave Bob Dragon's front door, come out again into Clyde Street and continue to walk west. A step or two on is St. Andrew's Cathedral, built for the Roman Catholic Church in Glasgow some 160 years ago. I should explain that we have three cathedrals in this city. There is the Glasgow Cathedral, now the chief church of the Protestant faith in the town. There is St. Andrew's, where we have just arrived, for the Catholics. And there is the Cathedral Church of St. Mary's, in the West End of Glasgow, for the members of the Episcopal Church in Scotland.

On Clyde Street St. Andrew's Cathedral looks rather sombre. Inside the church it is a different matter. The memorial altar to Monsignor Munro is considered one of Pugin's masterpieces, and the whole interior gives an impression of magnificence.

We go on, past Ropework Lane, where once there actually was a ropework. The building of the railway line into St. Enoch Station destroyed it and some excellent parts of old Glasgow. But slums were also swept away, and our Victorian ancestors considered the whole exercise a Good Thing.

Soon we come to the most graceful bridge over the whole of the Clyde—the Suspension Bridge between Clyde Street and Laurieston Place. But, since it was built by the people on the other side of the river, we leave it until we have investigated the left bank from the Victoria Bridge. I trust you still recall the method I have chosen to cover this part of the river. We go on the right bank from one bridge to another, and then retrace our steps and tackle the left bank from the same bridge to the next one. Here I propose a change. The Suspension Bridge is a pretty diversion. I don't count it as a real bridge. So I suggest we go straight on to Glasgow Bridge, the natural end of our chapter, before we return to Victoria Bridge and try the other side. Right? Right!

The Suspension Bridge is now part of the new look of the riverfront at this point. At one time there were low drab wooden buildings on either side of it, and you could see the river only by walking onto the bridge. A street to the right leads to St. Enoch Square, once the air terminal for Glasgow but now a mixture of shops, offices, a bus station, and a former hotel. This is yet another area destined for redevelopment, but just how it is to be redeveloped has not yet been decided.

Perhaps St. Enoch requires some explanation. It sounds like some sort of Midlands ancient archbishop. St. Enoch, believe it or not, is a corruption of St. Thenew, and St. Thenew was the mother of the patron saint of Glasgow, St. Mungo. At one time, long, long ago, the St. Enoch burn ran down through the square, which didn't exist then, of course, and joined the Clyde. On the bank of the burn was St. Thenew's Chapel. Its approximate position today is the Custom House, a rather dignified late Victorian building in Clyde Street. It's odd, by the way, to think that St. Enoch Square was, right up to the beginning of the nineteenth century, the central place for hiring sedan chairs. Glasgow streets were very dirty then, and nice people travelled by sedan chair.

We've looked up into St. Enoch Square and we go on now, past the Custom House to one of Glasgow's newest hotels, the 'Royal Stuart', and Jamaica Street. And here we are at Glasgow Bridge, sometimes called Jamaica Bridge because of the Tobacco Lords' street that leads to it. The Victoria Bridge is built on the site of the original Glasgow Bridge, but for many years Glaswegians have disregarded it completely and have given all their devotion to this bridge which runs between Jamaica Street and Bridge Street. There is nothing particularly remarkable about it. It's just that this bridge has wormed its way into the affections of the citizens, until they feel that it represents, somehow or other, the essence of the River Clyde as it flows through Glasgow.

We'll come back to it from the other side, for now we return to Victoria Bridge, cross it into the Gorbals and start a new safari. I should explain that the Gorbals was originally quite a small district on the South bank of the Clyde, but when it was raised to notorious fame adjacent parts were included by enterprising newspapermen who realized that, in the parochial air of Fleet Street, anything to do with the Gorbals was news and therefore saleable. So the Gorbals grew and grew, and today even Glaswegians are rather uncertain as to the precise area of the Gorbals.

The district has changed completely and, indeed, is still changing. It was still the old Gorbals when, on two occasions, I took Russian students there and once when I conducted Sir John Betjeman on foot. The Russian students kept on asking when they were going to see the Gorbals. When I explained that we were in the Gorbals, they flatly refused to believe me. The streets were too wide. The houses, though dingy, seemed respectable. They knew that I was part of some capitalistic plot and that I was out to delude nice, quiet, reasonable Communists. Mind you, if I'd stopped the bus and taken them round the back of some of these respectable-looking houses, they'd have seen a very different sight. I mentioned this to them, but they still thought they were being had.

It was rather different, naturally, with John Betjeman. We walked across the river and I decided not to tell him that we had now arrived in the Gorbals. We went down South Portland Street, which was then a wide thoroughfare with the remnants of Victorian respectability shoulder to shoulder with Sikh temples and Pakistani shops. There were even traces of the Irish and Jewish inhabitants who lived in the Gorbals and helped to make the place famous.

After a while Mr. Betjeman said to me, "When do we get to the Gorbals?" I was delighted to be able to tell him that we'd been in the Gorbals for the last fifteen minutes. However, I then took him to Gorbals Cross and explained that this was the only part of Glasgow where you could be certain that you would never have your pocket picked.

It is possible in Glasgow for a detective or policeman to arrest a man on a charge of 'being a known thief'. If this sticks, he can get quite a considerable sentence in prison. Well, 'known thieves' occasionally want to live a normal life, and so the pickpockets made a secret agreement with the Glasgow police that there would be one part of Glasgow where they would guarantee never to pick a pocket, if the police, in their turn, would guarantee never to arrest anyone on the 'known thief' charge.

You may not find anyone in the Glasgow police today who will admit to this secret agreement, but the point is now merely academic. The old Gorbals Cross has almost disappeared and, by the time these words appear, there may be an entirely new Gorbals Cross with no traditions whatever.

Gorbals, though just across the Clyde, had nothing to do with Glasgow for many years. For long enough the original bridge was known on the Glasgow side as Bishop Rae's Bridge, as if the Gorbals had contributed nothing to its erection. Perhaps this was somewhat due to the fact that Lady Lochow, the landowner on the south side of the Clyde, had founded St. Ninian's Hospital for lepers there. It was built on an ancient piece of land known as

St. Ninian's Croft and is commemorated today in Hospital Street.

Along the river from the Victoria Bridge you come to Gorbals Church, designed by one of Glasgow's best architects, David Hamilton. You don't see it at its best, however, since it was struck by lightning some years ago and part of the kirk, including much of the spire, had to be removed for safety's sake.

Then you arrive at Carlton Place, one of the Victorian show-pieces of Glasgow, a city which is regarded by international architects as having the finest Victorian buildings in Britain. Carlton Place is all that remains of a great scheme devised by the Laurie brothers. They bought a large part of the Gorbals and renamed it Laurieston. They worked out elaborate plans for a section of the South side of Glasgow that would at least equal if not be superior to anything in the building line on the north side of the Clyde.

They named the streets on their plans after English noble-men—Scottish noblemen were not considered quite good enough. That is why in the Gorbals today you have street names like Portland, Cumberland, Norfolk, Suffolk and Bedford, all dukes who would have been rather surprised to see the places put up in their names. For the Laurie brothers' scheme did not work, and instead of Laurieston becoming a well-to-do neigh-bourhood it started off as a mixture of middle-class and working-class buildings and tenements and went steadily down as little works and factories were introduced. Gorbals was still on its own, and the Glasgow authorities did not have the right to apply their rules to what was built on that side of the Clyde.

So all that remains today of the Lauries' idea of grandeur is Carlton Place and the Suspension Bridge. In their day Carlton Place was regarded as so exclusive that a gate was placed at either end, with a porter to see that only those entitled to use the place were admitted. Over the years business interests crept in, and some parts of Carlton Place were changed for the worse. But it's remarkable, in view of Victorian vandalism, how much was preserved. The pride of Carlton Place is the Laurie mansion in the middle of the terrace. It is owned by Glasgow Corporation and is well worth visiting for its fine ceilings, doors and other decorations.

There are gardens between Carlton Place and the river and in the Spring and Summer the flowers on the South side look across at the fine new promenade which has so brightened the scene on the North of the Clyde.

The Suspension Bridge, the most beautiful of all the Glasgow bridges, was built in 1853, when there were still hopes that Laurieston would become a fashionable area. It cost a halfpenny to cross the bridge and that meant that it was rather exclusive. A halfpenny was quite a sum in 1853, and why should you spend it crossing this bridge when all you had to do was to walk to the Victoria Bridge on one side or the Glasgow Bridge on the other?

Keeping to the left bank of the river, we walk along to Glasgow Bridge and the end of this chapter. This is the third bridge crossing the Clyde at this point. The first was the Broomielaw Bridge, opened in 1768. Glasgow Town Council engaged Thomas Telford to build a new bridge at the same spot in 1836. They liked the design so much that when it was necessary because of increasing traffic to build a third bridge in 1899 they asked the architect to give them a bigger replica of Telford's bridge.

This has always been the busiest and the best-liked bridge over the Clyde. Further down the river there are the George V Bridge and the new high Kingston Bridge, but neither has taken the place of Glasgow Bridge in the hearts of Glaswegians.

It's difficult to say which has been the biggest event in the life of Glasgow Bridge. But it's likely that two occasions have seen the bridge more crowded than it has ever been before. One was the time in 1962 when tram-cars disappeared for ever from the streets of the city. A procession of trams, ranging from an example of the first horse-drawn cars to the latest models, ran through Glasgow and across Glasgow Bridge to the Transport Museum at Eglinton Toll. More than 250,000 people turned out to see the end of the trams, and a great many of them watched the procession cross Glasgow Bridge.

The other occasion was in 1927 when 'Miss Anne Dapenny' arrived at Glasgow Bridge after having swum the Atlantic! This was a Glasgow University students' stunt to publicize their Charities Day. For a couple of weeks before the great day the Glasgow newspapers had been carrying stories of how this courageous damsel was swimming the Atlantic in order to be in the city for the celebration which bore her name. (Say 'Anne Dapenny' out loud, and you'll get the point.)

When she showed signs of flagging in her long swim, she was fed with nutritious haggis, and there was a piper in the little motor boat which accompanied her to play rousing airs and encourage her to greater efforts. These accounts were enjoyed immensely by the Glasgow newspaper readers, to whom student stunts were something new. Accordingly, when it was announced that Miss Anne Dapenny would actually reach Glasgow Bridge at the conclusion of her marathon swim at 11 o'clock on a certain morning, the citizens wanted to be in on the fun.

I was one of them. I remember dashing from my chartered accountant's office down to Glasgow Bridge to see the fun. It was a bitterly cold January morning, but up the Clyde chugged a motor boat with Miss Anne Dapenny thrashing nobly behind it. 'She' was actually a male student and was being towed by a rope.

The motor boat came into the Glasgow Water Police pier, and the valiant swimmer emerged to great cheering. Then Miss Anne Dapenny mounted a decorated motor lorry and was driven through the still cheering crowds to a place where restorative beverages could be supplied.

Everybody on Glasgow Bridge and around the Broomielaw enjoyed the stunt immensely. The local newspapers carried stories and photographs about it, keeping the students' story going. But Glaswegians were somewhat surprised to read next day in the national dailies printed in London and Manchester that Glasgow had been "hoaxed". These newspapers announced that huge numbers of Glasgow people had rushed to Glasgow Bridge because they believed that a girl had actually swum the Atlantic.

The question still remains as to who was hoaxed by whom?

A tug comes up river by a Clyde shipbuilding yard (overleaf) John Brown's yard, where the Queen Elizabeth II *was built. The town of Clydebank is on the right*

CHAPTER XI

"GLASGOW MADE THE CLYDE..."

I have already indicated that the popular local saying, "Glasgow made the Clyde and the Clyde made Glasgow", is not strictly true, since Glasgow existed long before its citizens paid any particular attention to the river. Even up to the time when Glasgow University was founded in 1451, Glaswegians looked upon their city as an inland town and the Clyde as good for salmon and a bit of a nuisance to cross.

It was all right if you didn't mind getting your feet wet. Where Glasgow Bridge stands today a boy could wade across the river at low tide even 200 years ago. The Clyde, as I say, stood for salmon, and there is an old tale that all apprentices in Glasgow businesses and shops had a clause in their indenture to protect them from being fed with salmon more than twice or thrice a week. This is a very good story, and you will still hear it in the town. But I regret to say that historians have been examining the indentures of Glasgow apprentices for years and have never come across even one with a clause about serving salmon too often.

The salmon story is still kept alive by the Govan Weavers, farther down the Clyde. When they held their annual dinner they had salmon, boiled eggs and "white wine". (The "white wine" was a euphemism for whisky!) The Govan Weavers still hold their dinner during Old Govan Fair each summer, but now it's boiled eggs and whisky, with sandwiches instead of the salmon. Since 1875 Govan has been famous as the farthest place up the Clyde for a salmon to reach. Now the work of the Clyde River Purification Board is obviously having effects. In 1973 a

John Brown's across from the entrance to the River Cart in to which big ships were launched

salmon was taken from the Clyde at Braehead Power Station, not so very far from Govan.

Even more remarkable, a salmon was caught in the River Kelvin, a Glasgow tributary of the Clyde, in 1967. I'm assured that the only way a salmon could get into the Kelvin would be from the Clyde, so that the Govan claim is now outdated. It has been said that, with a cleaner Clyde, it might be possible one day to catch salmon from Glasgow Bridge. That day may be coming sooner than we think.

Perhaps before we leave Glasgow Bridge and go down the Clyde, I should say more about how "Glasgow made the Clyde". Glasgow, as I have explained, was an ecclesiastical and university town, but the merchants could not be kept down. As far back as 1566 they realized that they could improve their trade if they could deepen their river. But nobody in authority would listen to them, and the ports lower down the Clyde—Dumbarton, Greenock and Irvine—kept growing and flourishing.

Scotland and England were united when James VI of Scotland became the monarch of Great Britain in 1603. But the two countries administered their own separate laws and parliaments until 1707, when the Act of Union was passed and the Mother of Parliaments first met in London. In that year the Glasgow merchants realized they must have a port. All the Clyde trade was going through Greenock. So what should they do? They decided to build their own harbour next door to Greenock, and they called it Port Glasgow.

All this time they were trying to work out how to deepen the Clyde as far as Glasgow itself. James Watt was consulted and made measurements and suggestions. Other eminent engineers were brought in. But it was not until 1768 that John Golborne, an engineer from Chester, produced a scheme for deepening the Clyde. It was passed and Golborne went ahead. He started by dredging the river. He built breakwaters, walls and jetties, and where some islands were in his way had them removed. He finished the job in 1775 and by that time he had deepened the Clyde even more than he had promised. The Glasgow magistrates were delighted. They gave Golborne a complimentary dinner, a silver cup and an extra £1,500 on the contract price.

This is how Glasgow started to make the Clyde into what is really a tidal canal from Glasgow Bridge down to Dumbarton. The Clyde Port Authority, formerly the Clyde Navigation Trust, carries out John Golborne's work today. They never stop dredging and deepening, and the river is now more than thirty feet deeper than it was in 1768. Over the years Glasgow has poured millions of pounds into the Clyde and got tens of millions back.

The view from Glasgow Bridge down the Clyde is severely curtailed. Right in front of you is the railway bridge taking the lines into the Central Station. No so long ago there were two railway bridges here and you will see the supports of the one which was removed still standing. In early Victorian days the railway ran to the south side of the Clyde and did not cross the river. From the riparian point of view, that would still be a good thing. But the first wet dock, Kingston Dock, opened in 1867. Only small ships and puffers were able to use the Kingston Dock. Most people know of puffers nowadays because of the "Para Handy" series on television, but the new puffers are trim little craft carrying coal and other cargoes up and down the Western seaboard of Scotland.

Glasgow's oldest dock has now been filled in and the scene from the George V Bridge down the river is very different from what it was even three years ago. At that time the steamer *Queen Mary II* sailed every summer's day from the Bridge Wharf, now neglected and desolate, to the south of the bridge. Since the new Kingston Bridge was built, the only vessels you'll see above it are dredgers and sludge boats at work. These belong to the Clyde Port Authority. The silt that is lifted from the Clyde is taken far down the Firth and dumped in the deepest part of the estuary, off the entrance to Loch Long.

At the moment it's no longer possible to sail down the river to the Firth of Clyde. But there are plans to run a service of passenger launches in the style of the famous canal buses of Amsterdam. As far as seeing the river is concerned, buildings on either side deny access to the public for many miles. However, if I'm to present a proper portrait of the Clyde I must describe it from the water, with the hope that you'll be able to see it that way before long.

If we're sailing, we go under the Kingston Bridge, and on the north side of the river we see the Burns-Laird steamers and cargo boats which ply to Ireland. Then come the quays where new vessels are fitted out. On the south side is the big ore-discharging plant at General Terminus Quay. Ships bring in iron ore to this quay, where it is discharged and loaded into trains for the Lanarkshire steel works.

The biggest crane on the river is on the north side. It is the 175-ton fitting-out electric crane. Behind it, on Gilmorehill, you can see Glasgow University. The university was founded in 1451, and the Old College was on a site in the High Street. Towards the end of the 'Sixties a move to the west was approved, and the new university, designed by Sir George Gilbert Scott, was opened in 1870. Some people refer to the University building scathingly as 'wedding cake' architecture, but John Betjeman described it to me as "fun". I suppose it depends on one's sense of humour.

On the north side of the river is the now empty Queen's Dock. There are proposals to fill it in and use the site for building. One good suggestion is to make a big exhibition ground there, for Glasgow has always been famous for exhibitions. On the south is Prince's Dock, still in use. Sometimes, by special charter, the *Queen Mary II* sails from here down the river, but normally her voyages begin at Gourock. Next on the north is Yorkhill Quay, where Anchor Line Ships dock from America and India. At one time there was a regular Atlantic passenger service carried on from Yorkhill Quay. (Unfortunately the phrase 'at one time' has to be used all too often on this stretch of the River Clyde). Beyond Yorkhill Quay is a complex of buildings set on a hill. This is the Queen Mother's Hospital, together with the Royal Sick Children's Hospital.

We enter the long line of yards running from Glasgow to Greenock, which once built ships. It doesn't seem so very long ago that I wrote these words:

And now you hear the start of the Clyde symphony—described by a

Glasgow man as "a helluva bashin' noise". About one third of all the shipbuilding in Britain is done here—indeed, more ships are built here than in any other place in the entire world. During the Second World War the Clyde built nearly 2,000 ships, repaired over 23,000, and converted hundreds of others. That's to say they built or repaired at least thirteen ships a day for five years. And they are still building the biggest and the best ships in the world here.

Brave words—and true words then! But things have changed and the Clyde shipbuilding industry is no longer as important as it was then. The ships are still the world's best, though the biggest are now being made in Japan. But a number of the shipbuilding yards have been closed down, and firms have found it necessary to form consortiums to keep the industry going at an economical level. As for the "helluva bashin' noise", it has almost disappeared because of new methods of building ships.

You will still see the names of the individual yards painted up on buildings and boards, although the yard is now empty or has changed to an entirely different use. I mention some of them now, because they were famous names, known to everyone who is keen on ships and their making.

Harland and Wolff still operate in Belfast, but not in Glasgow. They had seven berths and could build up to 75,000 tons of shipping a year. The buildings behind the yard are part of the Burgh of Govan. Since 1912 Govan has been part of Glasgow, but patriotic Govanites do not regard themselves as Glaswegians. Govan houses the famous Rangers Football Club. It has its own cross. And it has the finest collection of Druidical and early Christian monuments to be seen in the whole of Scotland. This collection is displayed in the grounds and inside Govan Parish Church. Govan even has its own pier, as we shall soon see.

Across the river from Govan is the Burgh of Partick, another town that fought to the bitter end to retain its identity. But it was swallowed up by Glasgow in 1912, and in Partick Burgh Hall, not far from the Clyde, the Provost of Partick threw his robe and chain of office on to the Council table and said, "There they lie—the abandoned habits of the Provost of Partick!"

One of the Clyde's biggest tributaries, the River Kelvin, joins the parent water at Partick. The Clyde end of the Kelvin looks rather prosaic, but it is a river with many charms. It's now possible to walk the banks of the Kelvin in almost uninterrupted parkland for several miles. Not far from its mouth the Kelvin runs through Kelvingrove Park, with the university and the art galleries facing each other across the river. Glasgow Corporation Art Galleries, incidentally, house the finest municipal art collection in Britain. I once took a London art critic round it on a Sunday afternoon. He was amazed and finally asked incredulously, "Are all these paintings the originals?" They were.

Kelvingrove Park housed the big Glasgow exhibitions of 1888, 1901 and 1911. If you look at the water of the River Kelvin today you'll be surprised to know that, during those exhibitions, the Kelvin was used for aquatic sports, and gondolas sailed up and down the river. Indeed, there is a famous story of the discussion in Glasgow Town Council of the proposal to import six gondolas from Venice for the River Kelvin. One Glasgow Town Councillor got up and objected to the expense. "Why bring in six gondolas?" he demanded. "Why not just get a male and a female, and let them breed!"

The trouble with Kelvin today is that a number of industrial concerns farther up its banks discharge their effluent into the river. Steps are being taken to rectify this, but progress seems very slow. At one time there was an open-air exhibition of modern sculpture held on the banks of the river in Kelvingrove Park. Dr. T. J. Honeyman, the Director of the Art Galleries at that time, was outspoken about the effluent coming down the river. He proposed that there should be a notice saying, "Scum to See the Sculpture"!

Past the River Kelvin there are on the north the great granaries of Meadowside, with the cattle lairage alongside. The cattle are brought in from Ireland and fattened in Scotland for the British market. Opposite the granaries is another famous shipbuilding yard, Fairfield. It became the Govan Division of Upper Clyde Shipbuilders Ltd., the firm that kept hitting the headlines. Now, along with Stephen's of Linthouse, they are Govan Shipbuilders Ltd. If orders are good more than 10,000 men are employed in this one yard. Among the ships they have built were the battle-ship *Howe*, the aircraft-carrier *Bellona* and the liners *Transylvania* and *Letitia*.

Below the river at this point is the Clyde Tunnel, which has made such a difference to Glasgow's traffic problems. There are actually two tunnels for one-way traffic in each, and they are in constant use.

There is a group of three shipyards before the King George V Docks is reached. On the north side of the river there are Barclay Curle's and Connell's. On the south side there is Stephen's of Linthouse. Barclay Curle's annual output capacity in the good old days was 100,000 tons. Now it's a ship repair yard. Connell's, one of the oldest of the yards, launched famous sailing ships, such as the *Star of Alaska* and the *Abraham Rydberg*. It's now Scotstoun Marine Ltd., owned by the Govan Shipbuilders. Stephens of Linthouse could turn out 50,000 tons a year of liners, warships, cargo boats and yachts in its heyday.

The last of the Glasgow docks, the King George V Dock, is on the left bank. It was opened by King George V in 1931. Alongside it is the site for an even greater dock, but the plans have not been carried out so far, and the farmland contrasts oddly with the red brick of the Braehead Generating Station, run by the South of Scotland Electricity Board. The great chimney of the power station is said to have the broadest diameter of any chimney in Europe—but we are still awaiting confirmation from Russia! The lights on top of the chimney are to warn off aircraft approaching Glasgow Airport by night. Many of the tall buildings in this airt carry warning lights.

If you're fortunate enough to be sailing down the river, you are moving out of Glasgow when you reach Braehead Power Station. The boundary on the south is Braehead itself, but we actually sail along the boundary for a while, because the north end of Glasgow is not reached until we arrive at another power station, Yoker, also run by the South of Scotland Electricity Board.

Before we reach Yoker, however, we've passed Yarrow's shipbuilding yard on the north and have crossed the track of

Renfrew Ferry, one of the two remaining ferries on the Clyde. Naturally, this is one of the places on the river which can be visited and where there is a walkway on either side. From the steamer you can see the tower of Renfrew Town Hall to the south, and Renfrew is a place worth visiting. It is a small but very ancient town. On the road up from Renfrew Ferry to the south stood the Castle of Renfrew, and here was the start of the Royal House of Stewart, from which our present Queen is descended.

Walter Fitzalan came from Shropshire to the Scottish Court in the twelfth century. In 1157 King Malcolm IV of Scotland appointed him King's High Steward and gave him the lands of Renfrew. The office was a hereditary one, and the family first of all called themselves Steward, and then Stewart. At the Battle of Bannockburn in 1314, when Scotland achieved its independence from the English rule under King Robert the Bruce, a Walter Stewart was among the bravest of men on that brave day. The following year he married Bruce's daughter, Marjory. It was their son who became King of Scotland in 1370, and so started the Stewart dynasty, which was to include Mary Queen of Scots, Bonnie Prince Charlie, Charles I and Charles II and the present reigning family.

Marjory Stewart was killed in 1316 when she was thrown from her horse while hunting near Renfrew. Her tomb is in Paisley Abbey, and Paisley is not far from Renfrew. Indeed, until fairly recently Glasgow Airport was situated at Renfrew, but now it has been moved to Abbotsinch, which is part of Paisley. Renfrew was always close to the royal family of Scotland, and in the fifteenth century the heir to the throne was given the title of Baron Renfrew. It is one of the titles held by the Prince of Wales today.

Little remains of Renfrew Harbour. Once there was a substantial little shipbuilding business around these parts. Simons launched many small war vessels and harbour craft for all parts of the world. Next to Simons was Lobnitz, another famous Clyde name. Their big claim to fame was that they built the prototype Mulberry Harbour, which made the D-Day landings a success in

The Tail o' the Bank, where the River Clyde turns into the Firth of Clyde

Normandy during World War Two.

It is necessary, by the way, to utter a word of warning here-abouts. Many people, seeing the name Clydeside, imagine that it consists entirely of Glasgow. But Clydeside, of course, means the whole of the area from Glasgow down to the Firth, and it includes such contiguous towns as Renfrew, Paisley and Clyde-bank which have resisted the importunities of the City of Glasgow for years and have no intention of being swallowed up by Big Brother. They are fiercely patriotic and resent any assumption that they are part of Glasgow. This is especially true of Clyde-bank, where the local people, known as 'The Bankies', are forever contradicting the foul canard that the *Queen Mary*, the *Queen Elizabeth* and the *Queen Elizabeth II* were built in Glasgow!

All these famous liners were built, of course, in John Brown's shipyard, possibly the best-known shipyard name in the world. Though it must be said that during World War Two the *Queen Elizabeth* was transporting thousands of American soldiers from their country to Greenock, when one G.I. said to a British sailor, "Don't you wish your country could build ships like this?" One hopes that the British sailor didn't come from Clydebank, other-wise mayhem would undoubtedly ensue.

John Brown's is on the north bank of the Clyde. Just before we reach it, we see Rothesay Dock, which is named after another member of the Royal Family and not, as so many people suppose, after the town of Rothesay on the Isle of Bute in the Firth of Clyde. King Edward VIII (the Duke of Windsor) opened it when he was Prince of Wales. As I have said already, he had the title of Baron Renfrew, but he also bore the title of the Duke of Rothesay.

Then comes John Brown's, which is no longer a shipbuilding yard. It was the Clydebank Division of Upper Clyde Ship-builders but when U.C.S. was liquidated, it was taken over by the Marathon Manufacturing Co. of Houston, Texas. Now, instead of giant liners, they build oil rigs, drilling platforms and semi-submersible barges for North Sea Oil development. Even now people who see John Brown's for the first time wonder how an 85,000-ton liner could have been launched in such a narrow space.

The Queen Mary II, *one of the famous Clyde steamers, at Dunoon Pier*

When the first of the big Cunarders, the *Queen Mary*, was about to take the water, an English shipbuilder was heard to ask how it was possible for such a leviathan to be launched into "that trout stream". The only reason that any big launch was possible from John Brown's in the old days was the existence of the little River Cart, diagonally opposite the launching berths.

When a ship was launched from John Brown's she went into the Clyde stern first and actually went part of the way up the River Cart. Then she was brought back into the Clyde and canted round to her berth in John Brown's. It looked impossible until you saw it done.

Clydebank, behind John Brown's, is not an impressive town, although it has its pleasant parts here and there. But it is a town of great character, built on its tough inhabitants. During the last war the Nazis mounted their biggest blitz in Scotland on Clydebank. They practically wiped out the town. Only six houses in Clydebank were left undamaged. But not one single bomb fell inside John Brown's shipyard.

Most of Clydebank was laid flat, and the death roll was enormous. But the workers started back in the shipbuilding yard the very next day. Some of them managed to find new accommodation not so far away. A large number lived in the ruins of their homes, like troglodytes. They were building what was then the biggest ship in the world, the *Queen Elizabeth*. After its launching it was taken secretly down the Clyde by night. Clyde-built ships do their trials off the Isle of Arran, on the 'Measured Mile'. There was no opportunity for the *Queen Elizabeth* to do any trials. She sailed straight across the Atlantic to begin work as a trooper. Could there be a finer testimony to the term 'Clydebuilt'?

Yes, Clydebank is industrial and workaday, but there is an indomitable spirit about the place which gives it an attraction of its own. As I have said, 'The Bankies' are tremendously patriotic. A friend of mine voyaged in a cargo ship which sailed from the Clyde to Finland. The Chief engineer was a Clydebank man, and he had taken his young son with him as a cabin boy. One day they went to see a famous waterfall in a Finnish lake. My friend was captured by its beauty and turned to the cabin boy, who was standing beside him looking at the scene, and said, "Have you ever seen anything so wonderful?"

"Aye, not bad," replied the cabin boy, "but have you ever seen Clydebank Public Park?"

Across from John Brown's yard the River Cart leads up to the town of Paisley, a big and bustling place and another of the burghs which make it quite clear they wish no truck with the City of Glasgow. Paisley has a harbour of its own, but it can be used only when the tide is right and even then only by smallish ships. At one time there were regular Clyde steamer services from Paisley, but now the only time that a steamer comes up the Cart is when it has been chartered by the enthusiasts of the Clyde River Steamer Society for a special trip.

Paisley had also its own shipbuilding yard, belonging to Fleming and Ferguson and founded in 1878, but it was closed down after ninety years of good and substantial work. It had eight berths and an output of small passenger ships, tugs and dredgers.

Not far from the harbour is Abbotsinch, the new Glasgow Airport. The Glasgow–London air service is the busiest in the whole of Britain, and planes fly from Abbotsinch to the United States, Canada, Iceland and many parts of Europe. During the war the aerodrome belonged to the Fleet Air Arm and was known as H.M.S. Sanderling.

There are some fine buildings in Paisley, notably the twelfth-century abbey, but most of them were presented to the town by millionaires who made their money there. Paisley is the world centre for thread-making. It was known in Victorian days as the place of 'pirns and poets'. 'Pirn' is the Scottish word for a reel or bobbin. The only Paisley poet remembered now is Robert Tannahill, who followed in the Burns tradition and whose cottage is still preserved as his memorial.

From the mouth of the River Cart and John Brown's yard the riparian scene begins to change. On the north there are still works and oil tanks and buildings. But the south bank is returning to the pastoral scenes we saw at the beginning of the river. Over on the south is Newshot Isle, which is actually a peninsula.

It seems to be a favourite place for small elderly wrecks (I mean ships, not human beings), but the reason for them is that Newshot and the boathouses at Park Quay are relics of a scrap depot used in the last war.

At one time (that phrase again!) you could look north from Newshot Isle to see the largest clock face in the world. It was part of the Singer Sewing Machine factory and was almost thirty feet in diameter. But the factory has been reorganized and partly rebuilt, and the clock has disappeared.

Just past Old Kilpatrick on the north is the new Erskine Bridge which has replaced the famous old Erskine Ferry. The new bridge, which connects Dunbartonshire on the north with Renfrewshire on the south, has not found great favour with road users, principally because it is a toll bridge and many drivers feel it's not really worth the money.

Behind Erskine Ferry and to the west is Erskine House, now known as the Princess Louise Scottish Hospital for Limbless Sailors and Soldiers. The Erskine estate belonged to the Earls of Mar, and later Erskine House was the home of the Blantyre family.

Old Kilpatrick is alleged by the Scots to be the birthplace of St. Patrick, the patron saint of Ireland. The Irish dispute this, but the Scots 'prove' it by pointing out St. Patrick's Well in Old Kilpatrick. There is a local legend, or, rather two local legends of how St. Patrick would have been happy to remain in Scotland if he had not been so sorely beset by the De'il. He decided to flee to Ireland, to get out of the tempter's clutches. When the De'il saw the saint escaping down the river, he wrenched a rock from Dumbuck Hill, just behind the village, and threw it at St. Patrick.

This is where the legend divides. One story is that the great lump of stone missed St. Patrick and is now Dumbarton Rock. The other is that the rock wasn't quite as big as that and that it, too, missed the saint and fell into the Clyde. That is why there is a large stone in the middle of the river with the name "St. Patrick's Stone Light" painted on it. There is a guiding light on the top.

Many Roman remains have been found in and around Old

Kilpatrick. It was the Western end of Antonine's Wall, which ran right across Scotland to Falkirk and the Firth of Forth. This was as far as the Romans ever settled in Scotland, though some legions made foraging expeditions to the north. Antonine's Wall was built to protect the Romans and their friends from the very unfriendly Caledonians. There were continuous assaults upon it, and eventually the Romans withdrew from Scotland altogether.

Now we see Bowling Harbour on the north. It marks the western end of the now derelict Forth and Clyde Canal, which ran across Scotland more or less on the line of Antonine's Wall. It took twenty-two years to build this waterway and it was known first of all as the Grand Canal. It started at Grangemouth on the Forth, and when it was officially opened on 28th July 1790 a hogshead of water from the Forth was symbolically poured into the Clyde. The length of the canal was thirty-five miles and it was extensively used by fishing boats, yachts, barges and even an occasional midget submarine until it became unprofitable. Much of the canal remains because its water is still used for industrial purposes.

Four different forms of transport can be seen at Bowling side by side. Placed so close together that you could throw a cricket ball over the four are the road, the canal, the railway and the river.

It's still difficult to get to the riverside on the north bank. Next to Bowling Harbour is a big oil-storage depot and it's not easy to make out Dunglass Castle nestling among the tanks. The castle belonged to the Colquhouns of Luss, and Robert the Bruce is said to have slept there; but little of the original castle remains and it is built into a charming mansion house, in which some of the rooms and furniture were designed by that famous Glasgow architect, Charles Rennie Mackintosh.

What you have no difficulty in making out is the obelisk in memory of Henry Bell. Bell is the man who is supposed to have introduced steam navigation to Europe, although, strangely enough, a steamer called the *Charlotte Dundas* was tried out on the Forth and Clyde Canal at the Grangemouth end long before Henry Bell's *Comet* first ran in August 1812. The *Charlotte Dundas* was a stern-wheeler, and it towed two loaded sloops along the canal for nineteen-and-a-half miles. In spite of a strong wind, a mere six hours was taken for the voyage.

I have already mentioned the steamboat experiments at Dalswinton Loch, much farther up the Clyde. There were Clyde-side engineers working on the idea of the steamboat, and there were experiments in both America and Russia. Henry Bell's claim to fame is that he made a practical go of the steamboat. In 1811 he had the Baths Hotel at Helensburgh (still there under the name of the Queen's) and he wanted to encourage trade. He thought he could get more people to come to Helensburgh if he ran a boat from Glasgow.

So he got his wooden ship, made by John Wood at Port Glasgow and put in an engine and a boiler manufactured in Glasgow. He named the result the *Comet* after the much talked about comet of 1811. Many wise people gave the ship no chance at all and suggested that travelling aboard the *Comet* would be positively dangerous.

But in the *Glasgow Chronicle* of 14th August 1812 Henry Bell published an advertisement which read:

The Steamboat 'Comet'. Between Glasgow, Greenock and Helensburgh. For passengers only.

The subscriber, at much expense, having fitted up a handsome vessel to ply upon the River Clyde from Glasgow, to sail by the power of air, wind and steam, intends that the vessel shall leave the Broomielaw on Tuesdays, Thursdays and Saturdays about mid-day, or such an hour thereafter as many answer for the state of the tide, and to leave Greenock on Mondays, Wednesdays and Fridays in the morning to suit the tide.

The elegance, safety, comfort and speed of this vessel require only to be seen to meet the approbation of the public, and the proprietor is determined to do everything in his power to merit general support.

This advertisement included the fares for intrepid passengers. The best cabin was four shillings per trip, and second class was three shillings. The *Comet* had a crew of eight, including a piper, and her skipper was William Mackenzie, a Helensburgh schoolmaster.

Captain James Williamson, the great authority on Clyde steamers of the past, wrote in his book, *The Clyde Passenger*

Steamer, about the *Comet* in these terms: "She was the first vessel moved by steam which successfully carried on a regular service in Europe, 13 years before the opening of the first public railway."

The remains of the Long Dyke can be seen in the river. This was one of John Golborne's successful ideas to confine the river current and deepen the bed of the Clyde. The dyke as it stands today, runs from Dunglass down to Dumbarton Rock.

Dumbuck Hill is to the north, with a great quarry eating into it. I wonder if this had anything to do with the legend of the De'il tearing a rock out of the hill and throwing it at St. Patrick? Between the Clyde and the hill are bonded stores containing whisky. These are guarded by a gaggle of geese which, according to the distillers, are better than any team of watchdogs.

This was the site of the original factory of Kosmoid Ltd., one of the great scandals of Scotland in Victorian days. Kosmoid was the invention of a Glasgow doctor, James Shiels, who claimed to be able to make gold from lead. He was so convincing that he persuaded some of the leading men of the West of Scotland to put their money into the project, and the name Kosmoid was supposed to be based on the initials of the 'angels'. K was alleged to stand for Lord Kelvin, I for Lord Inverclyde, one of the directors, O for Lord Overtoun, and the D for a member of the Denny shipbuilding family in Dumbarton.

The local town council were taken in by the ingenious Dr. Shiels as well and agreed with his proposals that they should build a new town on the top of Dumbuck Hill for the workers who would be needed to turn lead into gold on the shore of the Clyde. Then doubts began to arise among the investors in Kosmoid, questions were asked, and all of a sudden Dr. Shiels disappeared. He was never seen in Glasgow again, though stories were told of his having been seen begging in the streets of London. It is perhaps appropriate that there should be geese on the site where he did his 'experiments'.

Dumbarton Rock reminds many people of the Rock of Gibraltar in miniature. The rock is 260 feet high and a mile in circumference. The Romans are said to have occupied it because it makes a natural fortress. The Caledonians attacked it. And it is supposed to have been the site of some of the adventures of King Arthur and the Knights of the Round Table. Among others who attacked Dumbarton Rock were the Vikings.

Dumbarton Castle goes back to the Scottish Wars of Independence in the thirteenth and fourteenth centuries. Sir John Menteith, the traitor who betrayed Sir William Wallace to the English, was governor of Dumbarton Castle. On either side of the gateway are stone carvings of his face and Wallace's. You can tell which is Menteith because he has a finger in his cheek, the sign of a traitor. Wallace was imprisoned in Dumbarton Castle until it was time to take him to London for his 'trial' and execution.

Mary Queen of Scots has kept coming back like a song in this account of the River Clyde. She comes back once again for, when she was only 6 years of age, she sailed from Dumbarton Rock to France. Otherwise she would have been kidnapped by Scottish nobles who wanted the child in their power. She returned to Scotland and started her unhappy reign. I have already told something of her story. In 1568 she was fighting for her kingdom and only two Scottish castles—Edinburgh and Dumbarton—were left in the hands of her supporters. She was actually making for Dumbarton Castle when she was defeated at the Battle of Langside. But even if she had reached it she'd have found that it was already in the hands of her enemies.

One of the most daring attacks on Dumbarton Castle was by Captain Crawford of Jordanhill (now part of Glasgow). There seemed to be no way up the rock face, but the captain found a member of the garrison whose wife had been whipped by order of the governor for thieving. He wanted to get his own back, so he showed them a way up the rock. Captain Crawford's men went up using ladders and scaling hooks. Near the top one of the soldiers took an epileptic fit. His hands could not be moved from the rungs of the ladder, so the captain bound him to it and turned the ladder the other way round so that the invaders could keep climbing. The attack was a complete success.

Oliver Cromwell's troops occupied Dumbarton Castle for a time. In 1745 some of Bonnie Prince Charlie's friends were imprisoned there. Queen Victoria once held a court on the rock, and the British royal family have been visiting it ever since. There are two peaks. The view from the higher one, known as Wallace's Seat, is magnificent. You see right up into the Highlands, past Ben Lomond.

The river which runs round Dumbarton Rock to join the Clyde is the Leven. It comes from Loch Lomond, only a few miles away. At one time the loch was called Loch Leven, but the name was changed to the name of the mountain. Just behind the Rock there are the remains of a famous shipyard, Denny's of Dumbarton. Not far behind Denny's is a large red building. It is the second largest whisky distillery in Scotland.

Dumbarton is a busy little town, though some people call it 'the town that missed its chance'. It could have been the port of Glasgow. Glasgow Town Council suggested to the magistrates of Dumbarton in 1668 that this arrangement should be made, but the worthy bailies declined because they feared "the influx of mariners should raise the price of butter and eggs to the townsmen". It was soon after this that Glasgow made Port Glasgow on the other side of the Firth of Clyde. Then they gave up Port Glasgow because the river was deepened up to the Broomielaw. So Dumbarton could have suffered the same fate as Port Glasgow.

Dumbarton is a corruption of 'Dun Breaton', the fort of the Britons on Dumbarton Rock. But while the town is called Dumbarton, the country is known as Dunbartonshire. King Alexander II made Dumbarton a Royal Burgh in 1222.

There are only fragments of Dumbarton's history to be seen in the town. The broken arch of the Collegiate Church, founded in 1450, is near the Burgh Hall. In the main street you can see the old town house of the Earls of Glencairn. Admirers of "Dr. Finlay's Casebook" on television are interested in the fact that the author, Dr. A. J. Cronin, was a Dumbarton man. His first novel, *Hatter's Castle*, was set in the town. Cronin was actually born in Cardross, not far from Dumbarton, but practised as a doctor in the burgh. The "Levenford" of *Hatter's Castle* is Dumbarton, and the "Garshake" is Cardross.

CHAPTER XII

THE FIRTH OF CLYDE

The Clyde as a river finishes at Dumbarton Rock. Then it widens into the Firth of Clyde, which is really a miniature sea, with 1,240 square miles of salt water, great fiords among Highland mountains, a group of beautiful islands, and, on the Lowland side, long sandy shores backed by famous links which has caused this part of the Firth to be dubbed 'the Golf Coast'.

But no one in Scotland thinks of the Clyde as the river only. The Firth of Clyde is so famous that I have felt it necessary to devote a final chapter to it. Otherwise, many people would consider they had been cheated!

The best way to see the Clyde is from the water, if you can arrange it. True, the road on the east or Lowland coast is in sight of the Firth for most of the way, and there are some magnificent views from it. There are coast roads on the Highland side too, but long lochs penetrate the land, and road travel, though ever rewarding, takes a long, long time. There is a Clyde river fleet which includes a number of car ferries, so that it's possible to combine road and sea travel in almost all parts of the Firth.

The Lowland side still has a country aspect and just past the village of Langbank there is a mansion on the hillside. It is Finlayson House, where the Earls of Glencairn lived. The Earl of Glencairn in 1556 was the first Scottish noble to become a Protestant. John Knox preached at Finlayson House and dispensed Communion there.

As you approach Port Glasgow you see stumps of wood sticking out of the water. These are relics of the days when Port Glasgow did a big timber business with America. The posts show where the timber ponds once stood.

Across the water the Dunbartonshire shore curves slowly round to the Gare Loch by Cardross and the promontory of Ardmore. Robert the Bruce died in Cardross Castle in 1329. He became very fond of the Clyde and had little ships built at Dumbarton so that he could sail about the Firth. Some fanciful writers have described him as the first Clyde yachtsman for this reason. Others say that by building these little ships Bruce laid the foundations of a Scottish navy.

Not even the foundations of his Cardross Castle are to be seen today. The ground on which it was built is still called Castlehill and it was given to the National Trust for Scotland by Robert Cunninghame Graham, author, patriot and notable horseman. A memorial to 'Don Roberto' stands on the hill. It is a cairn twelve feet high, and it includes not only a portrait of Cunninghame Graham but also one of the horse which he rode for twenty years without a fall.

If you want to see the Gare Loch (the name means 'short' loch and it is only six miles long), you must go by road. There is a very occasional cruise up the loch, and motor boats and yachts use the few piers and jetties which are still available. Despite strong local feeling, the steamer pier at Craigendoran, between Cardroes and Helensburgh, has been closed to the regular Clyde fleet. Craigendoran had the advantage of being reached direct by rail from Edinburgh but voyagers from the capital must go by train to Glasgow now and then change for Gourock.

This is the entrance to the Gare Loch, and just ahead is Helensburgh, the 'model town' of the Clyde. Sir James Colquhoun eighth baronet of Colquhoun and Luss (and ancestor of the present Sir Ivar Colquhoun), decided to turn a little clachan named Milligs into a proper town, which he named after his wife, Helen. It was to be an industrial place, and advertisements were put out to attract weavers and bonnet-makers. But no weavers or bonnet-makers turned up, and in 1802 Sir James changed his plan and decided to make it a residential town built on the lines of the New Town of Edinburgh.

So Helensburgh is laid out mathematically on the side of a hill, and the people who live on 'The Hill' have nothing to do with the day trippers who flock down by rail and road from Glasgow and keep to the promenade and the shore.

Henry Bell, who sailed his *Comet* to Helensburgh, has a monument on the front in his honour, and in his lifetime he was honoured by being made Helensburgh's first provost (anglicé— mayor). J. L. Baird, the pioneer of television, was born in the manse of Helensburgh, and his boyhood friend in the town was Jack Buchanan. Another film star, Deborah Kerr, spent her youth in Helensburgh.

From Helensburgh up to Garelochhead the scenery is, to put it politely, mixed. This very sheltered loch was used in World War One by the Admiralty as a testing place for submarines. After the war came the Depression, and the Gare Loch became a kind of graveyard of the British Merchant Navy. Rusting hulks could be counted by the dozen. World War Two made the Gare Loch important again, and the War Office, the Admiralty and the American Services all took their own part of the loch shores.

The army and the navy are still there, and parts of the road north are so fenced in with wire that you can imagine you are in some sort of enormous concentration camp. And yet every now and then, as at Rhu for example, you come upon an unspoiled piece of the Gare Loch and can't even see the damage which has been done to the amenities. Rhu is the headquarters of the Royal Northern Yacht Club, the fifth oldest yacht club in the British Isles. Yachting is an immensely popular sport everywhere on the Firth of Clyde.

Above Garelochhead is Whistlefield, and here you can look down the Gare Loch on one side and on Loch Long and Loch Goil on the other. Mercifully, the signs of 'civilization' are absent in the Gare Loch view, which looks just as magnificent as the Lochs Long and Goil.

From Garelochhead you can take the road down the other side of the Gare Loch, past a string of little villages to Rosneath and then Cove and Kilcreggan. The delights of this road have diminished because it is the way to Admiralty stations on Loch Long, so that there is a deal of heavy traffic. But Cove and Kilcreggan are still very popular with West of Scotland business men, who come straight across the Firth by steamer from Gourock and use the road only when they must.

And now we cross the Firth of Clyde to Port Glasgow on the south. As I have said, the Glasgow merchants tried to get Dumbarton as their port. When they were refused, they built their own port in 1668, just three miles from Greenock, which was the most important port in the Clyde. They built the first graving-dock on the Firth here in 1762. Port Glasgow seemed destined to flourish—until John Golbourne of Chester deepened the river and the *Harmony* of Liverpool, a brig of 120 tons, sailed right up the Firth, past Port Glasgow into the river and docked in Glasgow in 1806.

But Port Glasgow, now deserted by the Glaswegians, kept going. It became highly industrialized and recked not of its appearance. So today it looks a rather drab place, although it must be said that the view *from* Port Glasgow is wonderful. Shipyards surround the only ancient building in the town. It can be seen from the water, but is not to easy to find in Port Glasgow itself.

This is Newark Castle. It is an old stronghold of the Maxwell family, who lived there until the beginning of the eighteenth century. The man who sold the Glasgow merchants twenty-two acres of land to establish their port in 1668 was Sir Patrick Maxwell. The castle, if you can find it, is open to the public.

Behind Port Glasgow harbour is the big red building which belongs to Gourock Ropeworks. You may recollect that I mentioned the firm already in connection with the work at New Lanark, a long way up the river from here. The reason for the firm's name is that it did start in Gourock, but removed to Port Glasgow. Gourock Ropeworks have not only made ropes for every kind of use, including the ropes for the great Clyde liners, but also made the big tops for the touring circuses in their great days.

There is a line of shipyards (including the famous name of Lithgow) and harbours leading from Port Glasgow to Greenock and you can see the new dock which the *Queen Elizabeth II* just got into and no more. We seem to glide imperceptibly from

Port Glasgow to Greenock. The yard and buildings and works show no transition from one town into the other. You should note the oldest shipbuilding yard in the world, Scott's. It was established in 1771 and the first vessels launched here were fishing boats. Now it is in a combine with Lithgow's.

On the river-front there is also the dignified aspect of the Greenock Custom House and the not so dignified aspect of the now dismantled Prince's Pier. This was a V.I.P. (Very Important Place) during the last war. The great Heads of State of the Western World knew it well because the Tail o' the Bank was the meeting place for the free world's fleet. Sir Winston Churchill and Roosevelt, de Gaulle and Sikorski, and other leaders, all visited Prince's Pier.

The Tail o' the Bank is a famous anchorage in the Clyde. The name signifies the end of a long sandbank which stretches under the water across the Firth. Today you will see big ships at anchor there, either to embark or disembark passengers to Greenock. Inward-bound ships going up the river also anchor here to await a suitable tide. During the war the great convoys mustered at the Tail o' the Bank, and troops from America, Canada, and many other places landed at Prince's Pier to set foot for the first time in Europe. They still come back to Greenock on holiday, though, as the years go by, in decreasing numbers.

Greenock looks better from the Firth than it does when you are in the town itself. It climbs quite impressively up a hill, and the tall Italianate tower is part of Greenock Town Hall. It was severely blitzed during World War Two, and new building is still going on. Greenock is industrial, like Port Glasgow, and has depended in the past on 'ships and sugar'. But it also had a distillery on the hill. In one of the blitzes a direct hit was scored on this distillery, and the inhabitants of Greenock had to watch with horror a river of flaming whisky running down the slope through the town and then into the Clyde.

Greenock, like most of the Firth towns, was originally a small fishing village. The local laird, Sir John Schaw, got a group of supporters together and pressed for Greenock to be made into a burgh. This was granted in 1707 and resulted in steadily growing prosperity. Greenock was the main port on the Clyde, and the town became so rich and influential that the Greenockians promoted a bill to establish a university there. But they were not quite influential enough, and the bill was turned down.

Greenock was the birthplace of a man mentioned several times in these pages—the great inventor, James Watt. It was also the birthplace of the infamous pirate, Captain Kidd. Hamish Mac-Cunn, a highly regarded Scottish composer ("The Land of the Mountain and the Flood" is his best-known work) was born here. So was Jean Adams, who is believed to have written that often sung "There's nae luck aboot the hoose". John Davidson, the tragic poet, was another Greenockian, and so was George Blake, the chronicler of the Clyde and author of the many "Garvel" novels, *The Shipbuilders*, *The Constant Star* and *The Westering Sun* among them. "Garvel", of course, was Greenock.

John Galt, the novelist and Empire builder, was born in Irvine, but he lived and died in Greenock, and there is a memorial to him in the town. And Burns enthusiasts remember Greenock because Highland Mary, whom he wed bigamously, died and was buried there. We shall see her statue when the steamer sails into Dunoon, where she was born, on the other side of the Firth.

Gaelic scholars have one thing in common—they invariably disagree with each other as to the origin of place names. Glasgow is a case in point. But there are two main theories for the name of Greenock. One is that it comes from 'grian', the sun, and 'cnoc', a hill, so that it means 'the sunny hill'. The other side says that it's 'Grain-aig', meaning 'a sunny bay'. Well, we know that the weather has changed over the years, but it must have changed especially in Greenock, for it has the reputation of being the wettest place in the West of Scotland.

From Prince's Pier you go past Fort Matilda and the dignified West End of Greenock to Cardwell Bay and the Clyde's chief steamer base, Gourock. Up on the Lyle Hill above Greenock, and overlooking Gourock, you see the Cross of Lorraine. It is a memorial to the sailors of the Free French Navy who sailed from the Clyde and died in action in World War Two.

There is generally a lot of action around Gourock. Steamers sail in and out from the pier, and ships are moving up and down the Firth. There are ferries criss-crossing the Clyde, and the pilots of the Clyde Pilotage are going out in their busy wee boats to board incoming ships or outgoing ones.

When we reach Gourock Pier we are out of the industrial area of Port Glasgow and Greenock, although the three towns are contiguous. Gourock is residential and can also lay claim to be a holiday resort. For people who want to have a holiday sailing on the Firth of Clyde, it is one of the best bases.

Gourock is built round Kempock Point, and just behind the pier is the Kempock Stone, known as 'Granny Kempock'. It stands on a little hill surrounded by tenements, but it is what remains of an altar to Baal in Druidical times. Although Greenock for many years was the most successful port on the Clyde, Gourock was a port before Greenock. Sailors and fishermen who came into Greenock believed firmly in the powers of 'Granny Kempock'. They would dig up some earth from around the stone and put it in among the ballast. This meant their ship was safe from evil. Others marched round 'Granny Kempock' seven times, carrying baskets of sand and chanting an incantation for a fair wind and a safe voyage.

This part of the Clyde was a famous place for witches. Farther down the Firth Robert Burns wrote of Tam o'Shanter and the witches' dance in the Auld Kirk of Alloway. In 1662 at a trial in Gourock a young girl named Mary Lamont confessed that she was a witch and that her coven of the Devil and twelve witches had planned to uproot 'Granny Kempock' and throw the stone into the Clyde. Thereby they would destroy the good that Gourock did to sailors. Having confessed, Mary Lamont was burnt at the stake, along with several other women whom she implicated.

The chief cruising steamer, the *Queen Mary II*, starts her sails at Gourock, the headquarters of the Caledonian Steam Packet Company, who own her. She begins by crossing the Firth to Dunoon on the Cowal coast. Steamers and car ferries go from Gourock to almost all parts of the Firth of Clyde. Although we see only the openings to Loch Long and the Holy Loch to the

"Highland Mary" on Castle Hill, Dunoon
Ruined Rothesay Castle

North, there are vessels going from Gourock up both these fiords and to Loch Goil as well.

The mountains which divide Loch Long from the Holy Loch are known as 'Argyll's Bowling Green'. This is supposed to show what terrific men the Dukes of Argyll were. They played bowls along the mountain tops! But it's believed now that the popular name is a mistranslation from the Gaelic. That may be, but it will be a long time before this scene is called anything else but 'Argyll's Bowling Green'.

Loch Long runs for twenty miles up to Arrochar, and Norwegians feel quite at home here. The mountains run down steeply to the water. If you sail up Loch Long you'll see the white hotel and the wee kirk alongside it that mark Ardentinny, of which Sir Harry Lauder used to sing:

> O'er the hill tae Ardentinny,
> Just to see ma bonnie Jeanie.

Today Harry Lauder wouldn't see only his bonnie Jeanie. He'd look across Loch Long to Coulport, where the Admiralty ballistic-testing station is sited, along with other odd erections.

Much of the mountainside around here is covered by State forests, which have taken away, to some extent, the majesty of the fiord-like scene. At Bird Point Loch Goil opens from Loch Long. Visitors are apt to assume that this is the Loch Goil mentioned in Thomas Campbell's poem, "Lord Ullin's Daughter". But the poet's Loch Goil is off the Isle of Mull. The steamer sails up the loch by the ruins of Carrick Castle, which was considered impregnable until the men of Athole took it from the Campbell clan in 1685. It's said that the first castle was built by the Vikings. But it's also said that it was built by Robert the Bruce when he was Earl of Carrick.

Lochgoilhead is a pleasant little village at the top of the loch, and it owes much of its charm to the fact that it is so remote. At one time it was immensely popular with day trippers, for the late Lord Rowallan gave his Ardgoil estate of 15,000 acres to the city of Glasgow to be used as a public park. For many years there were regular sailings to Ardgoil, but their popularity died out, and in

Rothesay Golf Course, with the "Alps" of Arran in the background

recent years the Corporation of Glasgow sold the estate to the Forestry Commissioners. Now the pier has been demolished. In spite of this, the loch has regained some of its popularity. It is a centre for West of Scotland Sea Scouts and other youth organisations and in the height of summer the water can be very busy at weekends.

Going up Loch Long we see the occasional train peching* up the West Highland Railway, one of the most scenically beautiful rail runs in the world. Below the railway is the oil port of Finnart, where enormous tankers come in to unload and the fuel can be carried right across Scotland by pipeline. Signs of 'civilization', however, are in the minority. The land is wild, and it's difficult to believe it was once well populated by the MacFarlane clan. They were as wild as the country and were so given to marauding by night that the local saying was, "The MacFarlanes have the moon for their lantern." Just across from Finnart at one time there stood some 200 houses. But they were pulled down at the time of the Highland Clearances, and the people went to Canada to make room for sheep.

At the top of Loch Long there is Ardgarten, the first caravan camping site in Britain, an Admiralty torpedo-testing station and the pier at Arrochar. Straight across from Arrochar is one of Scotland's most famous mountains, the Cobbler. From the village you can see the figure of the cobbler bending over his last, right on top of the mountain. The Cobbler's real name is Ben Arthur and, though it is a mere 2,891 feet, some of the most difficult climbing in Europe is to be found here.

All this can be seen on summer cruises from Gourock. But we are still aboard the *Queen Mary II* crossing from Gourock to Dunoon. Between the entrance to Loch Long and the Holy Loch, we see Strone Point. Strone comes from a Gaelic word meaning a nose. It's said that if you draw a straight line from Strone Point in a south-westerly direction it won't touch land before Spain.

The Holy Loch is now an odd mixture of holiday places and the United States Polaris base. You can see the parent ship and other supply ships, and there are almost certain to be Polaris

* Breathing heavily.

submarines tied up alongside or cruising the waters.

A popular legend for the name of the loch is that St. Mungo wanted earth from the Holy Land to be placed in the foundations of Glasgow Cathedral. The earth was sent to Scotland, but the ship bringing it up the Firth of Clyde ran into such a storm that it took shelter in this loch. But the storm was too fierce and the ship sank. So, since the holy soil was at the bottom of the bay, it was called the Holy Loch. A little of the soil was salvaged and was taken to the spot now called Kilmun, where it was used in the foundations for the ancient church there.

Well, Kilmun means 'the church of Mun', and the more likely reason is that the Holy Loch was so called because St. Fintan Munnu ('Mun' for short), a follower of St. Columba in the sixth century, built his cell there. The church named after the saint is now a ruin. It was founded in 1442 by Sir Duncan Campbell of Lochow. He was the first Lord Campbell and was known as Duncan the Prosperous. The Dukes of Argyll are his descendants, and the mausoleum in the grounds is the burial place of the Argyll family.

From Sandbank, across the water from Kilmun, down to Dunoon there is a string of villages in an almost continuous line. Sandbank is famous for yacht building. Then comes Hunter's Quay, with the headquarters of the Royal Clyde Yacht Club, the centre of activities during the famous Clyde Fortnight in July, when yachtsmen from all over the world come to race in these waters. We sail in past the now disused pier of Kirn to Dunoon Pier itself.

Dunoon is one of the biggest of the Clyde holiday resorts. It has a population of 10,000 which goes up to 30,000 every summer. It celebrated its centenary as a burgh in 1968, but in 1822 it was described as "a small decayed village". It owed its rise to the fact that rich Glasgow merchants built their summer houses here and started the Glasgow fashion of going 'doon the watter' to the Clyde villages.

Above the Castle Gardens you see a castellated building which you might imagine to be Dunoon Castle. Actually it is Dunoon Town Council Chambers, and was originally the mansion of a

Lord Provost of Glasgow, James Ewing. Dunoon Castle stood on a rock in front of the mansion, and a few stones of it can still be seen. Just below it is the statue of Highland Mary, the love of Robert Burns. She was Mary Campbell and was born in a thatched cottage at Auchamore Farm, not much more than a mile behind Dunoon. When she went to work in Ayrshire she met Burns and they exchanged Bibles over running water. So they were considered married in the 'Scotch style'.

Mary left Ayrshire to see her parents in Dunoon. But she got only as far as Greenock when she took a fever and died. In the statue she is shown looking across to Ayrshire, where her lover lived.

The first castle was built at Dunoon in the sixth century. In 1300 it was known as 'the Capital Castle of the Lordship of Cowal'. Robert the Bruce's grandson drove out an English garrison and was so ably assisted by Sir Colin Campbell that, when he became King Robert II of Scotland, he made Sir Colin hereditary keeper of Dunoon Castle. This was the signal for a feud between the Campbells and the Lamonts, who had held the lands of Cowal until then.

The feud came to a head in 1646 when the Campbells tricked the Lamonts out of their defensive position in Toward Castle, to the south of Dunoon. They took their prisoners to Dunoon and hanged the thirty-six most important Lamonts. Some hundreds of others were shot and thrown into a pit. Their bones were discovered at the beginning of this century when a new road was being made.

It was after this that the Campbells moved the seat of their chief, the Earl of Argyll, from Dunoon to Inveraray, where the present Duke of Argyll lives.

The *Queen Mary II* sails down the Cowal Coast past the village of Innellan to Toward Point. The big mansion there is known as Castle Toward and should not be confused with Toward Castle. Castle Toward was built by another Lord Provost of Glasgow, Kirkman Finlay, and now belongs, appropriately, to Glasgow Corporation. The ruins of Toward Castle are among trees about a mile farther along the road, which leads to Loch Striven.

From Toward Point, we sail into what is called by tradition 'sweet Rothesay Bay', a tradition based mainly on a Victorian ballad of that name, said to have been written by an English lady tourist. We are approaching Rothesay, capital of the Isle of Bute. Behind Bute we can see, if the weather is propitious, the towering mountains of the Isle of Arran.

These are the two largest islands in the Firth of Clyde. Bute is much smaller than Arran, but its population is three times as big, and Arran, with the neighbouring islands of the Cumbraes, is administered from Rothesay. Bute is about fifteen and a half miles long, but the Round Bute bus tour covers only twenty three miles. This is because considerable parts of the island in the north and south have only paths and farm tracks.

Its temperature is so equable that Rothesay has been called the Madeira of Scotland. It has also been named the Isle of Saints because among the holy people commemorated by places names and chapel ruins are St. Blane, St. Brendan, St. Ninian, St. Cormac, St. Mary, St. Colmac, St. Marnock and St. Michael. Even an Italian island could hardly boast such an array.

Rothesay, a holiday resort with a high reputation, is an ancient place with few vestiges of its history. Some historians say that it was the first place on the Firth of Clyde to have a quay of any sort. There is no sign of the quay today, which is not surprising since it was an eleventh-century one, but there is a modern pier. Incidentally, when I mention Clyde piers I am not writing about the kind of pier which is popular in English holiday places. Clyde piers are, in the main, severely functional. One reason for this is that the water in the Firth is much deeper than in most English places, therefore the pier does not need to be so long. So there is no point in overloading it with cafés, restaurants, pavilions and the like. These are on the shore at the pier-head.

The pride of Rothesay is its ruined castle, behind the modern buildings which front the pier. It is surrounded by a moat and visitors cross a drawbridge to reach it. Rothesay Castle is said to have been founded in the eleventh century by King Magnus Barefoot, the Viking. It was repeatedly besieged, captured, retaken and burned down. King Robert II of Scotland, the man who

restored Dunoon Castle to his country, made Rothesay Castle one
of his principal residences and also made his son the Duke of
Rothesay, a title which Prince Charles holds today. This first Duke
of Rothesay became King Robert III and made Rothesay a Royal
Burgh in 1400.

The principal landowner of the island is the Marquess of Bute,
who lives at Mount-Stuart House, not far from Rothesay. There
is a strong paternalistic attitude by the Bute family to the island.
Near the castle is the old mill, where a cotton industry was
established in 1778. Our old friend, David Dale, kept it going for
some years, but it faded out when the West of Scotland lost the
cotton industry to India. The father of the present Marquess of
Bute revived the factory as a tweed mill, and Bute tweeds have
been used by leading fashion designers in Paris.

Out from Rothesay pier we see in front of us 'Rothesay's
weatherglass', otherwise Loch Striven. This is another of the
Firth's fiords, and it is said that, whatever the weather is like in
Loch Striven, it will be the same in Rothesay fifteen minutes
later. In the interests of accuracy I must record that I have seen it
pouring in Loch Striven but sunny all day in Rothesay.

The steamer cuts across Kames Bay, leaving Loch Striven on
the right. We turn into the Kyles of Bute, a dog-leg of water
running round the Isle of Bute from Rothesay Bay to Ardlamont
Point, which marks the beginning of Loch Fyne. 'Kyle' is the
Gaelic word for a narrow strait and, as we approach Colintraive,
the strait is only about half a mile wide. The name Colintraive
means 'the swimming narrows', and this was where the Highlanders swam their cattle across, going to or from the Isle of Bute.
There is a car ferry there now, and this is the road link between
Bute and the mainland.

Just past Colintraive there is a group of rocks known as the
Burnt Islands, and the passage is so narrow that visitors wonder if
the steamer can possibly make it. It's worth while choosing some
point of vantage on deck so that you can see what a close thing it
is.

You should also lift your eyes to the hills in front of you,
because there is the fine new road on the hillside running from

Dunoon down to Tighnabruaich. I have said that the best views of the Clyde are from ship decks. But I must contradict myself here. The view from a car or bus on that new road is one of the finest in the whole of Scotland. You look right down the Kyles to Rothesay Bay and beyond. And when I describe a view as the finest in Scotland, you can be assured that it is also one of the finest in the world.

Now the steamer turns round the north end of Bute, past Loch Riddon, and sails south. Over to the left, on Bute, there are the Maids of Bute. These are two boulders on the hillside painted to resemble two old ladies in Welsh dress. This part of Bute is wild and uninhabited, and nobody knows why this painting was first done or by whom. But it is kept up to this day.

So we come to Tighnabruaich, Gaelic for 'the house on the brae'. This house was a famous inn. And this is the half-way point of the *Queen Mary's* cruise. The other half is the voyage back to Gourock.

Down the Kyles of Bute there is Inch Marnock, the 'Drunkard's Isle', so called because the Bute people put their alcoholics there with a supply of food and water and left them for weeks to 'dry out'. Then at Ardlamont Point Loch Fyne opens up to the North, between Cowal and Kintyre, and straight ahead is the Isle of Arran.

Arran has been called 'the epitome of Scotland', because every kind of scenery known in this country can be seen in this one island, although the road round it is less than sixty miles in length. Geologists regard Arran as a geological freak, because almost every type of geological formation known in Britain can be found here. Mountain climbers dote on Arran because, although the highest mountain (Goat Fell) is just under 3,000 feet, the quality of the climbing is high. Holiday-makers rush to visit Arran, and every village has its quota of Arranites who say this one is by far the best.

So far we've covered the Highland side of the Firth of Clyde, albeit in a rather cursory fashion. We must see the Lowland side in the same quick way. For this big area we simply haven't the space!

We can see some of the Lowland side by steamer too, for there are boats from Gourock which go down as far as Ayr. The voyage takes you down much of the area which saw the Battle of Largs in 1263, a battle which could have ended in Scotland belonging to the Scandinavians. King Haakon of Norway brought a great fleet of Viking galleys into the Firth, and they lay from Loch Long in the north right down to the Isle of Arran in the south. King Alexander III of Scotland took his army to Largs, and there, when the Vikings landed, he attacked. He was considerably assisted by a wild storm which made havoc of the Viking fleet. The Scots won the Battle of Largs, and the threat to their sovereignty was over— for the time being, at any rate.

Largs is another seaside resort today, but on your way to it you will see Fairlie, famous in its day for its roses and yachts and its steamer pier. Now there is a N.A.T.O. base there, and a great deep harbour development which, against local protests, is going to alter the whole character of the area. Then comes the huge Nuclear Power Station at Hunterston. The steamer goes round Portencross with its twelfth-century ruined castle, into Largs.

Across from Largs, and reached by ferry and steamer, are the Great and Little Cumbraes. The Great Cumbrae is yet another holiday resort, although it is only three and a half miles long. Its principal place is Millport, and one of its attractions is the Scottish Marine Biological Station and Museum, where a local octopus is on view. In the Parish Church graveyard is the tombstone of the Rev. James Adam, who, in the early nineteenth century, prayed every Sunday for "the Great and Little Cumbrae, and the adjacent islands of Great Britain and Ireland"!

Now we go down by what has already been called the Golf Coast. From West Kilbride to Ayr there are twenty golf courses, an average of one per mile. From West Kilbride onwards the Firth is better surveyed by road, so we abandon ship and go down through Ardrossan, where there is a busy harbour and car ferries from Arran, Ireland and the Isle of Man, to Saltcoats, a holiday place, and Irvine, a go-ahead industrial town which is being turned into one of Scotland's 'new towns'.

All the way down now there are holiday resorts with industrial backgrounds. Troon has a shipbuilding yard, Prestwick has an international airport (the only fog-free one in Britain), Ayr is a busy county town and the headquarters of the Burns Country. All over this part of Scotland the name most often mentioned is that of Robert Burns. The birthplace of Burns is at Alloway, near Ayr, and it is visited by some 100,000 people every year.

The Ayrshire coast goes down to Girvan. Out from Girvan and just across from the Mull of Kintyre stands Ailsa Craig, that volcanic rock which qualifies as a mountain because it is more than 1,000 feet. It's also known as 'Paddy's Milestone' because it is half way between Belfast and Greenock, and it showed Irish emigrants that they were well on their way to fame and fortune in Scotland.

But Ailsa Craig is really the full stop at the end of the Clyde. And so, naturally, we finish there.

INDEX